# Praise for *the 5 Overwhelm Culprits*

"Corrie's powerful storytelling and practical advice make *The 5 Overwhelm Culprits* a must-read for any woman balancing the complexities of modern life. Her vulnerability is inspiring, and her framework is a lifeline for those seeking to turn their overwhelm into purposeful action."

—**Jess Ekstrom,** founder of Mic Drop Workshop, two-time bestselling author, and Forbes top-rated keynote speaker

"Corrie offers easy-to-absorb advice to help you release overwhelm, find inner peace and ultimately, create a life you love. Her vulnerability is real, raw, and inspirational. I highly recommend this book for any woman who's tired of trying to 'do it all.'"

—**Jaclyn Gallo,** TEDx speaker and bestselling author of *Stop Getting In Your Own Way*

"Corrie is a true powerhouse and an inspiration to women and leaders everywhere. Whenever I feel overwhelmed, I return to Corrie's lessons to guide me to the other side. Her approach is no-nonsense, and her insights are practical, inspiring, and actionable. This book is a must-read for anyone seeking to elevate their life."

—**Amanda Jefferson,** podcaster, Top 50 Women speaker, and one of the world's first KonMari consultants

# *the* 5 Overwhelm Culprits

# the 5 Overwhelm Culprits

## Strategies to Save Your Sanity Without Sacrificing Your Success

### Corrie LoGiudice

Health Communications, Inc.
Mt. Pleasant, South Carolina

*www.hcibooks.com*

Library of Congress Cataloging-in-Publication Data
is available through the Library of Congress



ISBN-13: 978-07573-2610-3 (Paperback)
ISBN-10: 07573-2610-2 (Paperback)
ISBN-13: 978-07573-2611-0 (ePub)
ISBN-10: 07573-2611-0 (ePub)



Publisher: Health Communications, Inc.
1240 Winnowing Way, Suite 100
Mt. Pleasant, SC  29466

Cover, interior design, and formatting by Larissa Hise Henoch

*For my children—*
*so you never learn to confuse*
*exhaustion with success*

# Contents

# Foreword

"Leaders don't create followers—they create more leaders." Tom Peters said this years ago, and it is one of my favorite quotes, as it's one of the clearest definitions of what embodied and trustworthy leadership truly is. It's also the heartbeat of what Corrie is doing in the world with her speaking, coaching, and now writing, especially in this book.

I met Corrie several years ago, when she enrolled in my business mentorship program. I remember that she was coming out of a very turbulent time of life. Within just a few sessions, I watched something shift. I witnessed purpose-driven passion, a soul calling that snapped in place. Corrie has a rare ability to discern through all the world's noise and stay aligned to her path—especially when life is difficult, uncertain, and demanding. She learns from everything she has been through and even more amazing is her ability to let it refine her; that is the secret path to staying steady and not falling into panic or overwhelm. This kind of steadiness, of inner certainty and steadfast confidence, is earned through incredible life experience, and I've seen it up close.

When Corrie later shared that she wanted to write a book and we began working together in my author program, I saw the deeper layers of her work and the place she leads from: The evolution, her integrity, and the focused care she brings to every aspect of her work are how she is able to render this work so smoothly. This book is a continuation of who she already is—someone who leads from lived experience, grounded clarity, and a deep respect for the reality most women are silently suffering in, alone.

If you're holding everything together right now—your work, your home, the people you care for, and concerns about your future—this book will feel like a supportive friend who gets you when the rest of the world feels judging. Corrie has finally named the truth of what we go through without victimizing or blaming ourselves. Instead, this is about rising into the leader within yourself to take control of your life and live in integrity with who you are meant to be.

Many women are expected to be exceptional everywhere, all the time, all at once. We're asked to lead professionally and then keep leading when we walk back into our personal lives, where the invisible labor is waiting and the emotional load doesn't ever stop. Add grief, trauma, loss, divorce, miscarriage, caregiving, financial pressure, politics, world affairs, and the countless "life events" that arrive at the worst possible time, and it's no wonder so many high-performing women feel like they're drowning in plain sight.

Having spent much of my life *overgiving* and trying to be everything for everyone while losing myself, I know how important and powerful it is when a book comes along with the language that can help us make sense of our patterns—because understanding where we've been is what allows real change to begin. More importantly, tools like the ones in this book help us understand where we've been so we can choose what comes next. We are no longer just letting life happen to us, being bumped around like bumper cars; we hop in the driver's seat and steer ourselves forward out of stress, chaos, and overwhelm. So here are your keys to the open road ahead.

Corrie gives you a framework you can actually use—one that helps you identify what's driving the overwhelm and where to begin, without requiring a perfect schedule, unlimited resources, or a complete life overhaul. The wisdom here is practical, lived-in, and something we all can find comfort in.

You'll find stories that are honest and transformative in a memorable way. I invite you to open this book the way you would begin a road trip—with curiosity, presence, and a willingness to see what reveals itself mile by mile.

Corrie embodies and teaches us that leadership is not only a role you hold in the world—it's the relationship you build with yourself and choices you make each moment. Page by page, you're being invited back into your own discernment, clarity, and capacity to lead your life from the inside out.

The change starts with us. I'm grateful you're here, and I'm proud to support Corrie in placing this book in your hands.

**—Shannon Kaiser,** bestselling author of *The Self-Love Experiment* and founder of She Saves Herself Collective

# Introduction

I don't know about you, but I'm so exhausted I'm pissed off.

As women, we're expected to be everything to everyone. A sampling of all the things I've been expected to be in my life, all at the same time, includes:

- Daughter
- Sister
- Niece
- Granddaughter
- Friend
- Student
- Partner / Wife / Divorcee / Widow (depending on the year)
- Provider
- Mother
- Caretaker
- Housekeeper
- Scheduler / Organizer
- Driver
- Bill payer

- Cook
- Shopper
- Survivor (for me, miscarriage, abuse, divorce, *and* suicide loss)

I've been expected to be all of this, in addition to being a high-performing:

- Employee
- Manager
- Boss
- Leader (again, depending on the year)

I'm sure you have a list of your own. Although it might be different from mine, we are joined by a common thread: We are modern-day super women, slowly drowning in a sea of unrealistic expectations slapped together with a lifetime of recurring tasks and traumatic life events that happen to all of us at exactly the WORST TIME EVER, because we're so busy trying to live up to the deadlines and expectations our bosses and families have set on us that we do not have time to deal with "life." Ever.

Back when I was going through five years of hell on earth (see the "survivor" bullet above), trying to balance my career as a senior vice president with unimaginable life crises, I searched high and low for any sort of resources that could help. Courses, books, blogs, *anything*. My goal with this book is to fill the cavernous gap of information that search revealed.

Of course, there are many self-help books on the market on numerous topics. For instance, you can find tons of resources on how to improve your personal life. You have opportunities to master relationships, homemaking, your marriage, parenting, your finances, among others. Visit any bookstore, and these books might fill up half the shelves.

Resources on improving your professional life are everywhere as well. Books on training and courses on leadership, management, sales, marketing, operations, and more professional topics than I could count fill up the other half of the bookstore.

Where the hell are the books that help you navigate the responsibility of having to hold everything together, both personally and professionally?

Where are the books that help you continue to lead when you leave the office and your personal life is waiting for you, slowly burning to the ground when you get home? And, worse yet, you're the one expected to lead your family out of it.

Spoiler alert: There are none. So back in the day when I was commuting an insufferable twenty hours a week, I added audiobooks, podcasts, and online courses from both categories into my listening queues to try to figure out how in the world I was going to survive for the long term.

Women are expected to lead two very different and separate lives. Along the way, I've learned that being an effective leader requires diligence in both categories. If you can't think clearly because you're sleep deprived, your diet is terrible, and your exercise schedule is nonexistent, it's going to cause you undue stress, affecting not only your direct reports but, worse yet, your children. Being effective in both contexts requires a full-person solution.

At the time of this writing, the top ten ranked leadership and motivation books are written by men. Historically, men don't have to wear half the titles I listed above in addition to their professional roles. So when pivotal life events get thrown their way, they have more capacity to manage it and still lead effectively. Hell, according to the Hays Gender Diversity Report 2017, 24 percent of men were promoted after having children, compared to only 10 percent of women.[1] The so-called fatherhood bonus is very real, whereas the motherhood penalty predicts the child's mother will struggle to advance her position in the workforce.

We as women don't have the luxury to forego our careers when we become mothers, and this uneven treatment can adversely impact our personal relationships, as well as our mental and physical health. Unfortunately, this won't change until more women push their way into leadership roles and change the antiquated systems driving society today.

I've identified the Overwhelm Culprits—the lack of Clarity, Confidence, Community, Conditioning, and Consistency, all the things that cause us to feel like we are in a losing battle with life—after being challenged by my longtime therapist (who you'll hear more about later in this book) to figure out a way to teach other people how I successfully managed my own overwhelming life scenarios while still continuing to professionally outperform peers as a leader in my career.

I turned my lessons into a framework to neutralize these offenders, and I've been sharing this remedy onstage for audiences across the globe for the past five years. At the end of every keynote, where I hold a meet-and-greet, I get asked if I have a book on the topic. I'm excited to offer this book to you: a resource women in or aspiring for leadership can keep on their bookshelf and refer to when needed.

A few quick notes to be aware of prior to us continuing on this journey together. The first is I've made an effort to make the examples shared in this book as relatable as possible. The solutions I mention can be used by anyone, in any situation, regardless of gender, race, and financial position. Whereas many books on similar topics are written by women in a place of privilege, including access to things like live-in nannies and outsourcing everything under the sun, you'll soon see it's not about access to money. You can achieve so much by utilizing mindset alone.

In addition to sharing stories and examples from my own experience having been a working single mother with limited resources, there are also stories and experiences collected from over a hundred working mothers from all walks of life. Some of the stories I personally share may be triggering if you've ever experienced trauma. I candidly share about my own miscarriage, surviving an abusive relationship, and suicide loss; so if you are a trauma survivor, please be sure you are also working with a mental health professional in addition to utilizing what's shared in this book.

Names have been changed to protect the anonymity, not only of my research participants, but also members of my family who do not wish to be known publicly. You will also find supporting research and data to show you that you are not alone in what you are experiencing, as well as what needs to happen to improve your situation.

I recommend reading this book all the way through in chronological order for the best experience, but don't feel pressured to do all the actions and exercises in order. The beauty of the Overwhelm Culprit framework is that it meets you where you are today, in the current moment. It's also highly customizable. If your culprit today is Lack of Conditioning, it makes no sense for you to start off with Lack of Clarity solely because that's the first one featured in the book. So first give yourself a solid understanding of all five Overwhelm Culprits and then feel free to use this book as a reference manual you can refer back to anytime you feel overwhelmed once you can identify your culprit and know exactly where to start.

I truly hope this book plays a part in effecting change because there's one thing I know for sure: I didn't struggle to kick and scratch my way to the top and successfully overcome all the societal roadblocks in my way only to have my daughter have the same experience twenty years from now with zero support and resources, like I did.

The change starts with us. And knowing your Overwhelm Culprit will help you to keep taking action, no matter your circumstances, and have a part in that change.

Part One

# When Enough Is Enough

# Chapter One

# It Starts with You

*Try not to resist the changes that come your way.
Instead, let life live through you. And do not worry that
your life is turning upside down. How do you know the
side you are used to is better than the one to come?*

—Rumi

I just couldn't take it anymore, so the words poured out of my mouth: "I quit."

They rolled so easily off my tongue you would have thought they'd been rehearsed. But the truth was they were words I'd been terrified to say for months—one of the many sources of my overwhelming stress and anxiety encapsulated in just two words. I felt a wave of immediate relief the second I pushed them out.

My father responded, "So wait, are you *resigning*?"

I broke down into uncontrollable tears. The reason these words were so hard for me to say and why I had been avoiding them for so long is because the last thing in the world I've ever wanted to do was to hurt my father. I had just hit him with a verbal sledgehammer, and I felt awful about it.

Up to this point, I had worked for my family's company for over fifteen years. I was currently the senior vice president, my father was the president, and he had been grooming me, the third generation in our family, to take it over. I was his baby girl, the one he had trained to be a leader and a fighter in an entirely male-dominated industry, wholesale electronics distribution, and who did so effortlessly and with respect. Though he rarely ever said it to me directly, I knew how proud he was based on what everyone in our industry had shared with me. All too often I'd be on a business trip where a colleague would pull me aside and share with me how my dad shared with them about an out-of-the-box campaign I came up with, or the way I stepped in to save the company's self-hosted, self-destructing IT server when he was out of the country.

And here I was, throwing it all away with two small words that were loaded with meaning. I didn't do this in the confines of an office or after a meeting. This was on a cruise ship, during our annual family vacation. What precipitated this move? After we returned from a day of excursions and sightseeing, my dad and I returned to our suite to check our work email. In doing so, I absolutely lost my shit after learning he had undermined one of the business decisions I had made prior to leaving for the trip, impacting three of the departments I oversaw, in favor of a last-minute, received that day request from my male VP. This was someone who reported to me, but my father had spent as much time mentoring him over the years as he had me.

My reaction was not unwarranted, and these statistics bear out what women in the workforce face:

- Women make up 47.7 percent of the global workforce[2] but still earn $0.77 for every $1.00 earned by white men.[3]
- Despite outnumbering men in the U.S. college-educated workforce[4] and outperforming male counterparts in Fortune 200 CEO roles,[5] women hold only 27 percent of management positions and just 10 percent of CEO roles.[6]

Here I was, thinking I had finally made it to the top based on my own merit, only to discover my boss—albeit my father—trusted and respected the opinion of another man more than his own mentee and daughter. I snapped and quit on the spot. My father remained speechless and stunned, and it made for an incredibly awkward rest of our trip.

The rest of what followed is somewhat of a blur. All I remember is being at dinner at the fancy steak restaurant later that night, fighting back tears at a giant table filled with eight members of my family. My three-year-old son sat next to me, and I was completely incapable of making sure he had what he needed at that moment. Worst part is I knew it. I looked out the window of the cruise ship in desperation and thought: *It would be easier if I just jump off. It would save everyone the trouble of me being a giant disappointment.*

But it wouldn't be easier, and I knew this. Because not even three months earlier, my long-term, post-divorce partner died by suicide. I was the lucky one to find him.

Sadly, I'm not alone.

The irony of these inequities is that, despite us high-performing women showing up and performing at the top of our class in spite of the lack of respect, we successfully do so alongside navigating deeply personal challenges, not unlike my own:

- One in four women have experienced a miscarriage[7]

- One in three women have faced physical violence by an intimate partner[8]
- Half of all married women have endured divorce
- One in four women have lost a loved one to suicide[9]

These are not extraordinary crises. They are everyday realities women must shoulder while continuing to lead in the workforce, often without the time or space to process them.

So many of us working women find ourselves years later, swallowed alive by our careers yet buried in debt, not making anywhere near the money we were promised, paying out the vast majority of our salaries to cover childcare that's more expensive than our housing,[10] and still balancing the unpaid labor of running a household no different than the 1950s housewives did. Let's not forget the 23.4 percent of us in the sandwich generation, simultaneously providing caregiving for minors as well as elderly parents.[11] Unlike our male, non-caretaking counterparts, we don't have time to deal with the day-to-day tasks left up to us, never mind pivotal life events. When they do pop up, it adds even more stress and anxiety to an already maxed-out baseline, and we feel like we're drowning. This makes hearing news of your boss siding with your male direct report feel like acid being poured on an open wound.

Here I was only three months into debilitating grief, made even more complex by the fact that the love of my life had chosen to die, and here I was considering the same for myself because I felt so desperately unseen, unheard, invalidated, isolated, and on the brink of insanity. So much so I'd considered for a second my son's life was better off without me in it.

It's no wonder that, after the pandemic, millennial working women worldwide feel "stuck," and worse yet, like they're failing. And many women stay stuck because they don't feel safe enough to be vulnerable and talk about it, all due to the guilt and shame we carry for failing to live up to society's expectation of perfection that's constantly perpetuated in the media.

Having been curious about how similar my experience was to those of other working mothers, I later conducted an interview project where I spoke one-on-one to over one hundred women during the course of two years, asking them all about their pains, frustrations, fears, and challenges when it comes to balancing motherhood alongside advancing their careers. The responses to my social media posts and emails looking for participants were overwhelming in themselves. I was floored by the hundreds of comments with volunteers who were so desperate to have their experience be heard that they'd agree to hop on a thirty-minute Zoom call with me, a total stranger.

Looking at the data collected, it's easy to see we're not alone in this experience.

## Balancing Work and Family

When it comes to balancing work and family, 60 percent of mothers I've interviewed reported feeling torn between being a good employee and a good mom, struggling to balance both motherhood and getting work done. They also shared concerns that being a mom may hinder chances of promotion. Worse yet, they feared missing out not only on their child's important first moments but career advancement opportunities.

One story that stands out to me and still haunts me today is Melissa's. She was originally in the audience of one of my speaking engagements and later answered the call to participate in my research project. She broke down in tears, sharing how when she returned to work after her recent maternity leave, she was offered a demotion she didn't ask for so she'd "have more time to care for the baby." On the flip side, upon returning from paternity leave, her husband was offered a raise and a significant pay bump. The guilt and shame she carried from secretly resenting her husband's ascension through the ranks and her being left behind is heartbreaking. While she was happy to have the extra household income, the slight to her was unmistakable. Parenthood isn't a competition, but the inherent sexism in the workplace created a situation like this.

## Mental Load and Stress

Of the more than one hundred mothers I interviewed, 78 percent reported frustration with the mental load of managing both professional and personal responsibilities. As someone who's gone through this myself, it's a special kind of excruciation to go through your entire workday so excited to see your kids, only to then find yourself completely checking out mentally during their bath time to think about a report you have due the next day. When you are not 100 percent present in your surroundings, wherever you are, you feel like you suck at everything. The irony of this is that the majority of the women surveyed were high performers, and they knew they could perform at an even higher level if they had the opportunity to be fully present.

Their greatest fear was that they'd lose everything if they stopped: their status, flexibility, and, most importantly, security in their careers for themselves and their families. They're tired of feeling overwhelmed and burned-out due to high expectations and limited time. They also find themselves not leveraging flexibility at work when it is offered to fend off burnout and better manage their mental load for fear they will be judged or passed over for promotions, or they fear that they will lose the flexible positions they need.

One participant named Jen is a solo parent and partner at a law firm. Despite her company's generous vacation policy, she still found herself constantly responding to Slack messages from vacation or, worse yet, her son's baseball games. She was so grateful to have the flexibility to work remotely that she was terrified that it would be revoked if she set boundaries for her availability that differed from her older, pale, stale, and male colleagues. If that happened, she feared she'd have even less time than she already has with her son.

## Career and Ambition

When it comes to their careers and overall ambitions, 74 percent of mothers I've interviewed questioned if it's even possible to remain ambitious in their career while being a devoted mom. They cited challenges with societal structures that aren't set up for two working parents, high childcare costs, and inflexible company policies as being significant barriers to achieving the ambitions they set for themselves.

One mother named Amy has aspirations of reaching executive leadership at an organization in which both she and her husband hold leadership roles. She shared that she's approached multiple women executives for guidance and mentorship on how they got to where they are while also caring for children, only to be disappointed to hear they had all taken a leave of absence while their children were Amy's son's age.

She also felt devastated by her recent annual review when she should have felt overjoyed. She was ranked the top manager and made the most money but felt frustrated because it came at the cost of spending time with her seven-year-old son. She knows she has what it takes in order to ascend to a higher position, but with her husband having similar aspirations and not being willing to take on more responsibilities with their child, she's stuck at the level she's at.

# Childcare and Family

An overwhelming 76 percent of mothers I've interviewed cited high childcare costs as being a significant burden. It's not an overstatement to say this is reaching crisis levels. At the time of this writing, the cost of childcare in the United States exceeds the cost of housing in all fifty states.[12] The interviewees cited the lack of flexible childcare options as making it difficult to manage work schedules and family needs. Add to this the difficulty finding reliable and consistent support for childcare, and you now have many women feeling like they are forced to make a choice between their families and the careers they love.

And that's just finding care when your kids are healthy. We all know daycares can be germ factories, which makes balancing caretaking and work that much more complicated when kids become ill. Mothers are often either forced to take time off from work or send their child in anyway when they should be home resting (and not infecting other kids with their germs). Staying home with your child often means you then get sick yourself and are stuck in a position where you already used up a chunk of your sick time so you have to go to work, leaving you with no time to rest and take care of yourself. It's an awful scenario to be in.

Multiple women I spoke to had recently decided it was time to leave the workforce, despite not wanting to, for financial reasons. They find themselves handing over the entirety of their paycheck just to be able to go to work, and since they're making less than their partners due to the gender wage gap, guess whose job is more expendable?

This problem is not limited to the United States. Take the story of Victoria from the United Kingdom whom I spoke with. A mother of one with a second baby on the way, she continually brought up the costs of childcare as an ongoing pain point through our entire conversation. She shared that following nine months of paid maternity leave (far better than we receive here in the States), she came back to work in a part-time role. Although she aspired to move up into leadership, she feared not having the sufficient childcare support she would need to be able to perform in a higher-level role. Finding care for a sick child, in particular, especially when she doesn't have family close by, felt nearly impossible.

She's not alone. According to a 2021 State of Motherhood Survey conducted by Motherly, 56 percent of mothers felt they lacked "a village" they can call on for support.[13] Families often live farther apart. Grandparents, who in the past would have been available, might delay retirement and work into their later years to account for high living costs, not unlike their adult children. For women like Victoria, it's understandable to believe the only option you have when a second baby comes into the picture is to leave the workforce altogether.

## The One Thing

When I asked the participants what they felt was one thing they were missing:

- 20 percent reported *Time*
- 16 percent reported *Support*
- 14 percent reported *Peace of Mind*
- 12 percent reported *Balance*
- Others reported *Motivation, Clarity, Confidence,* and *Skills*

It's easy to understand their responses when it comes to time, support, peace of mind, and balance based on the systematic challenges shared in the statistics and stories above. It's worth noting the gaps when it comes to solutions for motivation, clarity, confidence, and leadership skills. According to leadership development firm DDI's 2023 Global Leadership Forecast, there are significant gaps in mentorship and transition support in setting up women for leadership success.[14]

As evident from my own research project, the majority of the women I spoke to were having difficulty finding mentors who had the same lifestyle situations they themselves have. So as much as they want mentors, the diversity needed at the top isn't quite there yet to get women the support they need. And when it is, it's often disappointing to learn of the sacrifices these women executives have had to make in order to be there, not unlike Amy's previously shared experience. Despite recommendations like those DDI makes about educating women on the importance of mentorship early in their careers, the problem isn't a lack of this awareness. They're looking, but they are not finding the right mentors. It's no wonder they aren't feeling motivated or have clarity, confidence, or the right skills.

The second missing element for success, which seems like it should be a no-brainer, is transition support. Without the right support during the vulnerable period of transitioning into a leadership role, it's less likely leaders will remain engaged and succeed in their roles long-term. DDI's research showed women were 12 percent less likely than men to receive any leadership skills training, and 15 percent less likely to have their leadership skills assessed to gain insights into their strengths and development gaps. Women are shortchanged in two respects: On top of the challenges women often balance in their personal lives at home, they also aren't receiving the support they need professionally to succeed and rise through the ranks at work.

Needless to say, this needs to change. According to the World Economic Forum, it's still going to take over 131 years to reach true gender parity.[15] Women are in crisis mode, and no one is coming to save us, yet we keep believing someone or something will. As children, every toy and story targeted to us girls reiterated the narrative that princesses are always saved by our princes, and all we had to do was trust, sit, and wait in the tower to be rescued. But if we keep on waiting, we'll all want to throw ourselves off the tower (or in my case, off the ship) to end the pain.

The solution is simple: Women have to take action and save ourselves. Not only for our mental and physical well-being, but also for the well-being of our families, colleagues, and communities. As the saying goes, the definition of insanity is doing the same thing over and over again and expecting different results.

If we want our situations to change, *we need to change.* We need to change our mindsets, our beliefs, our boundaries, and, most of all, our expectations. It's time to stop waiting for Prince Charming to fix the societal systems and instead place ourselves in positions to change them ourselves.

In the meantime, in direct opposition to what the burnout prevention gurus tell us to do, it's also going to require us taking on more rather than less responsibilities to effect change. Which is also why so many women in my research project shared that they resist personal and professional development—it's another thing to add to an already overflowing to-do list. The good news is the frameworks and tactics I'm going to share with you in this book are going to enable you to increase your capacity without sacrificing your well-being, by being strategic in where and how you take action. The million-dollar question is determining exactly where to start.

Circling back to that moment when I was on the cruise ship, the suicidal ideation I was having made me pause and think about what my partner must have thought moments before he made the decision that changed not only my own life but the lives of everyone surrounding him. If only he'd asked me—or the many other people who loved him—for help, I wouldn't have had to suffer the grief of losing him, the grief that made the pain of showing up to a career I wasn't fully invested in, commuting an ungodly number of hours daily to get to work, and missing my son grow up even harder to bear. I had finally reached my breaking point. I was overwhelmed.

Like the feelings I was experiencing in that moment and you may at one point have experienced too, overwhelm is a sign: **It simply means something in your current strategy needs to be accommodated to your current reality.** In my case, multiple things had changed in my reality.  I had lost my life partner, and I had lost the vision of what my future family was going to be. I had also lost the vision of my career path and my sense of self in the process. There were also many things I had gained, like my beautiful three-year-old son, who I wish I had more time with. My lifestyle as it was set up that day was no longer sustainable or compatible with my current life situation. It's no wonder I felt like I was going insane; I was living a life where my actions were directly conflicting with the values most important to me.

I didn't want my son or my family to suffer. I also knew I couldn't continue on the path I was taking, *and I had to make an effort to change myself.* So instead of jumping off the deck of the cruise ship, I called my therapist and prayed she'd help me find the clarity I was seeking. Because the truth was, if I was contemplating jumping off a cruise ship and plunging fourteen stories into the ocean to my death . . . I must not have a whole lot of clarity.

Even in the chaos of that moment, I was clear about one thing. Enough was enough, *and I quit.* Something needed to change, and that change was going to start with me. If you've picked up this book, my guess is you know this about yourself, too.

At this point, the case has been made that working women are more overwhelmed than ever. But unfortunately, we're also living in a time when our basic human rights are being rolled back at a rapid pace, which effectively means our daughters have fewer rights than our own mothers did. We need more women leaders, and we need them fast, so we can't just up and quit. We need to have plan.

The next step is drumming up the motivation, clarity, confidence, and skills to pick ourselves up, dust ourselves off, make the changes necessary to take charge and lead action, and rise up from the ashes like the badass phoenixes we are.

# Part 2

# Stop Settling, Start Leading

# Chapter Two

# Get Off the Hamster Wheel

*Sometimes you don't get what you want,*
*because you deserve better.*

—Unknown

One day, two years after my divorce but before the suicide loss, my therapist asked me a question that changed my life as I knew it—*forever.*

Ironically, I had no idea why I had signed back up to work with her again. My life at the time was everything I had ever dreamed of. I had finally become a mother—a longtime dream of mine. I had an incredible career, a six-figure income, and loved the work I was doing as well as the people I had the opportunity to do that work with. I had recently bought my first home, another lifelong dream, in an incredible school district. I looked and felt better physically than I ever had in my adult life. I was fit, light, energetic, and had a glow about me that people just couldn't help but stop and notice. I'd have fellow local moms, complete strangers to me, hit me up in my Facebook DMs sharing that they loved my "energy" and wanted to hang out, so my social life was buzzing once again. Post-divorce, I was head over heels in love in a healthy relationship with a man who treated me like a queen, shared the same life vision I had for myself, and had boys the same age as my son who became his best friends. We had even very recently discussed the prospect of moving in together and getting engaged in the next couple of months.

Yet despite all of this, I just could not shake this odd, unsettled feeling. When my friends would ask me about it, all I could respond with was that I felt weird. I'd ruminate about it every single evening on my long, mentally painful rides home from work (I'll share more about these commutes in Chapter 5).

Knowing how well my therapist, Elizabeth, had helped me navigate my contentious, high-conflict divorce, I enrolled myself back into therapy more than a year later to figure out what the hell I was feeling and why I wasn't happy.

That day, while sitting on the couch in her office, discussing my drive—not my commute, but my motivation—she asked me: "Corrie, have you ever considered becoming a coach? Like a life or a business coach?"

The question stunned me into silence. Because, if I was to be truly honest with her, I had.

Around three months earlier, while scrolling the offerings on Netflix for something to watch, I had accidentally stumbled across a documentary called *I Am Not Your Guru,* which followed a day in the life of the most famous life coach of all time, Tony Robbins. The rest of the world might have known about Robbins, but this was the first I'd heard of him. I was fascinated with everything about him: his business model, his commanding deep voice, his high-energy events, and even how he prepped for them by jumping up and down on one of those mini-rebounder trampolines.

In the documentary, there's a scene in which he asks the audience to raise their hand if they've ever felt suicidal. A couple of hands went up, and he approached one of them. I sat there, completely and utterly transfixed, as he asked this man a series of incredibly simple questions. I watched that man go from bawling and visibly carrying the weight of the world on his shoulders to laughing and then suddenly feeling so light and free that he couldn't help but jump up and down, smile, and shout with glee. To me, Tony came across as a modern-day superhero with the ability to help people see differently and rewire their thoughts. The energy he wielded in that room felt exhilarating, even though I experienced it through a television screen and not in person.

I had turned the TV off that evening, thinking to myself, *Holy shit! How amazing would it be to have a job like that?* only to find myself immediately dismissing it. It's easy to understand why I did so.

On paper, I had everything I had ever wanted: the house, the white picket fence, the kid, the amazing career, the man, you name it. I had it all, in addition to the expectations of a future already mapped out for me. I had spent over fifteen years being groomed to take over my family's business (more on that later as well). Either way, I figured I wasn't cut out to be a coach. I'd have no idea where to start, had no skills for it, and had already invested close to two decades in my current career.

When I snapped back to reality and realized that silence wasn't going to work as the answer Elizabeth was looking for, instead of answering, I asked her a question in return:

"No, why do you ask?" That's right, friends, I lied to my therapist —straight-faced—too afraid of telling the truth out loud because of what that would mean for me.

To which she answered, "Corrie, I work with a *lot* of patients. Many going through traumatic situations, but none like what you had gone through in your marriage. I've never seen someone in my professional career manage to handle the level of overwhelm, stress, and anxiety you went through and still accomplish everything you have in such a short time frame while also maintaining the capacity necessary to fully heal emotionally. If you could figure out how to teach people what you've managed to do, you could have a lasting impact on others. Being a coach would be a great way to facilitate that."

Her saying *"lasting impact on others"* hit me like a ton of bricks. The potential that I could be like Tony Robbins was seemingly terrifying in a way I didn't have the ability to pinpoint. It also meant that what she was not so gently nudging me to admit was that I was unhappy in my seemingly perfect life and career, and that's probably why I was feeling *weird*.

But here's the thing. I'd been running so fast on the treadmill of life that the thought of stepping off it to do something else was paralyzing. So instead of taking action, I chose to do nothing. It felt easier to just keep going through the motions, even if those motions no longer had the same effect they used to.

Let's dive deep into what causes this, why it happens, and what to do about it.

# Chasing Success

For years, I chased success in the way I and many others had been taught to understand it, by proving my worth through external achievements like promotions, accolades, and financial milestones, and each one felt like validation, a reassurance that I was doing everything right. Yet, underneath the polished veneer of success, I felt exhausted, disconnected, and quietly suffocated by the weight of expectations that weren't fully my own.

You know, *weird*. And I'm not alone.

As I began to work and speak with more high-performing women in my research, I noticed a pattern. So many of us had been conditioned to believe that success meant keeping up with impossible standards—being exceptional in our careers, present and nurturing at home, endlessly competent in every role we played. We internalized the belief that slowing down or shifting priorities would mean failure. And worse, we feared what it would cost us to question these definitions of success and lose the momentum we'd built.

This isn't just about work-life balance. It's about the invisible forces that shape how women see themselves and what they believe they are allowed to want. The illusion of success, the fear of disrupting the status quo, the deeply ingrained "good girl" conditioning, and the tendency to measure our worth by the wrong metrics quietly dictate our choices, keeping us in cycles of overwork, self-doubt, and hesitation.

# The Illusion of Success

Many women, myself included, build a life that looks great on paper or on social media, but feels empty in reality. The career, the home, the family, it's all there but something still feels off. Or if you're like me, you feel *weird*.

Society tells us that once we "check the boxes," we should be satisfied, but we don't talk about what happens when satisfaction doesn't follow.

Research participant Mitsuko had everything she believed she wanted: a high-powered career that paid well, a reputation as a strong leader in her field, and a life that, from the outside, looked like a success story. She had spent years climbing the ranks, putting in long hours, and proving herself, not only to herself, but to her hard-working, immigrant family. It was a priority to her to make them proud based on all the sacrifices they had made for her to reach that level of success.

But behind the polished exterior, Mitsuko was exhausted. Her to-do list never ended, and every attempt to scale back her workload left her drowning in guilt. She wanted to work less—to reclaim time for herself, her relationships, her health—but no matter how much she achieved, the pressure to keep pushing forward never let up. What made it worse was that she knew something had to change, but the thought of slowing down felt impossible. Success had become her expected identity—if she wasn't working at full speed, who was she?

The *illusion* of success is this: Society conditions us to believe that once we reach a certain level—whether it's the six-figure salary, the leadership title, the corner office—we'll finally feel satisfied. Yet so many women, like myself and Mitsuko, get there only to realize they're still unfulfilled, still overwhelmed, still craving something more. Worse, the fear of stepping off the hamster wheel keeps them stuck. They think, *If I let go, will I lose everything I worked so hard for? If I stop pushing, will I become irrelevant?*

But here's the truth: Success isn't about how much you achieve, it's about how aligned your achievements are with the life you actually want.

# Fear of Disrupting the Status Quo

Regina had spent years carefully building a career she was proud of. She had transitioned out of education after becoming a mother and found herself in the tech sector. She climbed the ranks, secured a stable role in a respected organization, and was on the verge of stepping into an even bigger leadership position.

On paper, everything was working. But inside, she felt stuck.

Burnout was creeping in. The long hours, the mental load, and the constant pressure to go above and beyond—it was unsustainable, yet the thought of stepping back or making a major change terrified her. It was not because she didn't want more balance; she did. In fact, she had already started setting stronger boundaries: logging off at 5:00 PM to pick up her kids and resisting the urge to take late-night calls just because someone else was in a different time zone. But even though her company was supportive, she struggled to let go of the expectation she had placed on herself to always be available.

Her biggest fear was that prioritizing herself and her family would mean losing momentum in her career. It was not unlike my own fear that pivoting to coaching would somehow roll back the fifteen years I had already invested into my SVP career.

Regina wanted to move from senior manager to director, but every time she thought about actively pursuing it, self-doubt crept in. *What if I'm not ready? What if I fail? What if I disrupt the stability I've worked so hard to build?*

This is the trap of the status quo. Even when we know something isn't working, the fear of disrupting what's familiar keeps us stuck. We tell ourselves it's safer to keep going through the motions than to risk the unknown.

# The "Good Girl" Conditioning

Alyssa had done everything right.

She'd worked her way up in health care, a notoriously male-dominated industry, and had just stepped into a high-stakes leadership role—helping launch a new heart surgery program. It was an incredible opportunity, one that most people in her field could only dream of achieving.

Yet she couldn't shake the feeling that she wasn't the right person for the job. At work, she worried she wasn't good enough. At home, she worried she wasn't doing enough. She spent her days pouring herself into both worlds, terrified of falling short in either.

When her contract was nearing renewal, she thought about negotiating. She had spent years proving her worth, demonstrating results, and leading with confidence. But when it came time to advocate for herself, the thought paralyzed her. *Maybe I don't deserve a raise,* she thought. *Maybe I should just be grateful I have this job at all.*

It wasn't until her husband bluntly pointed out, "This is why men make more money than women," that she realized what was happening. She wasn't doubting her abilities—she was doubting whether she had "the right" to ask for more. And that's when it hit her: This wasn't just about her job. This was how she had been conditioned to think her entire life.

For as long as she could remember, Alyssa had tried to be "good": a good student, a good employee, a good mom, a good wife. She did what was expected. She followed the rules. She never wanted to be seen as difficult, demanding, or selfish.

But that came at a cost. The guilt weighed on her daily. She felt like she was always falling short, no matter how much she gave. She dreaded taking time off for her kids, fearing her job would think she wasn't serious enough. She never once searched for work-life balance solutions because, deep down, she thought this was just the price she had to pay.

Alyssa wasn't alone in this. Women, especially those in high-performance careers, are taught to work twice as hard for half the recognition and to never, ever ask for more than what they are given. They are taught to be grateful, not bold; to be accommodating, not assertive; to give endlessly, even at the cost of their own well-being. And because of this conditioning, many women never realize they're settling.

## Identity Tied to the Wrong Metrics

Melissa, who we discussed briefly in Chapter 1, had always been a high achiever. In her early career, she climbed the corporate ladder with ease, and her performance reviews were filled with phrases like "top performer" and "high potential." She prided herself on her work ethic, often staying late and taking on additional projects. Success, to her, meant promotions, accolades, and the clear upward trajectory of her career.

Then she became a mother.

When Melissa returned from maternity leave, she quickly realized the workplace she had excelled in now saw her differently. Despite being told she was a top performer before she left, she was offered a demotion upon her return so she could have "more time with her baby," something she'd never even asked for. At the same time, her husband, who also worked at a large corporation, received a promotion. The contrast was stark and undeniable. Melissa was suddenly expected to take a step back while her husband was rewarded and encouraged to step forward.

Melissa struggled to make sense of it. Had she changed? Had her skills suddenly diminished? No. What had changed was the way her value was being measured. At work, she was now seen as someone with "divided priorities." No longer the employee willing to work long hours, answer emails at all times, and take on extra assignments, she was viewed as someone who was "managing" rather than "excelling." Even though she continued to perform at a high level, she wasn't seen as going above and beyond because her time *outside* work now belonged to her child.

At home, the internal conflict was just as strong. She felt immense guilt when she prioritized her work and an equal amount of guilt when she prioritized her child. She found herself measuring success by the wrong metrics, asking herself: *Was today a "good employee" day or a "good mom" day?* The idea that she could be both felt impossible, and with good reason. She was measuring herself based on everyone else's metrics as opposed to her own.

Her frustration wasn't just personal—it was systemic. Her employer never asked male colleagues with young children to prove their commitment. The expectation that she should either sacrifice her ambition for her family or push through relentless overwork to "prove" herself was an unwinnable game. And the longer she played by those rules, the more exhausted she became.

For women like Melissa, the pressure to tie their identity to external validation—titles, promotions, performance reviews—creates an unsustainable cycle. When those metrics shift after motherhood, it can feel like failure, even when nothing has actually been lost.

The key to breaking free from this cycle is by redefining success on your own terms. This means shifting from measuring your worth based on how much you do for others to measuring it based on how aligned your actions are with your values. Melissa didn't need to prove herself by overworking—she needed to reclaim her own definition of success.

For some, that might mean pushing forward in their careers with clear boundaries. For others, it might mean strategic pauses or pivots. But the most important shift is recognizing that your worth is not tied to an arbitrary metric designed by a system that was never built for working mothers to succeed in the first place.

## So, How Happy Are You, Really?

I'm going to ask you a question right now, and it's really important that you're honest with yourself, not just with me.

Are you happy in your life right now? On a scale of 1 to 10, where 1 is the worst and 10 is the best, how would you score your life?

Now, before you answer, let me clarify something—*happiness and satisfaction* are two different things. I'm not asking whether you're satisfied with where you are. Satisfaction is often tied to external markers—your achievements, your salary, your home, your family. What I want to know is whether you feel joyful and grateful to wake up in the life you're living.

According to the OECD's Better Life Index,[16] people worldwide rate their lives at an average of 6.7 on a 10-point scale. If you land somewhere around there, you're living what many would consider an "ordinary" life.

And that's part of the problem. Society tells us that an ordinary life is the goal. Work hard, hit your milestones, check off the boxes, and be grateful for what you have. But what happens when you do all of that and still feel like something is missing?

If you had asked me years ago, I would have said my life was a 9. I had the career, the home, the "success." But looking back, I now know it was really a 6.7. I wasn't unhappy, but I also wasn't deeply happy. And the reason I couldn't see that was because I was chasing a definition of success that wasn't my own.

Here's how to find out if the same is true for you. Review the list below of the ways we commonly settle but may not be aware of, and make note of how many ring true for you.

# Ways You Are Settling (but Don't Realize It)

Below you'll find sixteen different ways you may be settling. Review them and count how many apply to you today.

1. **You describe your life as fine, good enough, or okay.** If you're not excited about your life but also not miserable, you might assume you should just be grateful. But *fine* isn't the same as *fulfilled.*

2. **You often say, "I should be happy," but something feels off.** You have everything you thought you wanted, yet there's an unshakable feeling that something is missing.

3. **You get defensive when someone asks if you're happy.** If someone asked, "Are you happy?" and your immediate reaction is discomfort or justification, it's worth digging into why.

4. **You tell yourself, *It's too late to change now.*** If you believe you've invested too much time, energy, or money into your current path to change it, you're likely settling out of fear, not fulfillment. This is exactly what I experienced when considering the prospect of pivoting careers into coaching.

5. **You minimize your own dreams.** When you catch yourself thinking, *I've always wanted to do [X], but that's not realistic,*

you're likely settling for a version of life that's safer, not necessarily better. You know, the same reason I thought I could never do work like Tony Robbins.

6. **You work hard but don't feel deeply satisfied by your accomplishments.** If you achieve your goals but feel more relieved than fulfilled—or worse, immediately move on to the next goal without celebrating—you might be chasing external success rather than personal joy.

7. **You prioritize making others comfortable over making yourself happy.** If you consistently ignore what you want because you don't want to inconvenience or upset others, you're likely settling in ways you don't even realize.

8. **You stay busy to avoid thinking about your dissatisfaction.** A packed schedule might make you feel productive, but if you never pause to check in with yourself, you could be distracting yourself from bigger truths.

9. **You admire other people's lives but assume you could never have that.** If you look at someone living boldly and think, *Wow, that must be nice,* instead of *I wonder how I could create that for myself,* you're settling in your assumptions about what's possible.

10. **You feel guilty for wanting more.** If you have a good life by most standards but still feel like something is missing, do you immediately feel selfish, ungrateful, or guilty? That's a sign you're settling—and shaming yourself for it.

11. **You don't let yourself dream too big because you're afraid of disappointment.** If you only set goals you know you can achieve, you may be playing small to avoid potential failure or judgment.

12. **You stay in relationships, jobs, or situations because they are "comfortable."** Comfort can be a trap. If something isn't

bad enough to leave but also isn't truly fulfilling, you're likely settling.

13. **You convince yourself you don't have the time, money, or energy to change.** While practical limitations are real, if you use them to avoid even thinking about what you want, you're keeping yourself stuck.

14. **You rationalize why you can't have what you want.** Every time you start to dream about a different life, do you immediately list reasons why it wouldn't work? That's a sign you're shutting yourself down before you even try.

15. **You assume change is too big, so you don't even start.** If you believe you need a complete life overhaul to be happy, you're likely missing the small steps that could bring more joy today.

16. **You haven't checked in with your childhood dreams in years.** If the younger version of you could see your life today, would they be excited or confused?

Experiencing one of these doesn't necessarily mean you're settling for less, but if you're experiencing more than one, that's a big red flag that it's time to evaluate what it is you really want in life, regardless of what anyone else thinks.

The last one regarding your childhood dreams can be super insightful when you take the time to sit and analyze it. Let's dive into that next.

## Reconnecting with Your Inner Child

There's a question everyone gets asked as a child: "What do you want to be when you grow up?" Do you remember what your answer was? I wanted to be the first female director to win an Oscar. Obviously, that didn't happen. I allowed someone I trusted to talk me out of it, and I'm not alone.

Almost half of middle-aged millennials wish they had chosen a different career path.[17] Even worse, 48 percent of them said their parents strongly influenced their career path, and 40 percent of them felt pressured to follow their parents' career advice.[18] Unfortunately, the trend isn't stopping with this generation.

Look at the following 2021 survey conducted by YouGov.[19] Kids today have job options available to them that we, as millennials, never did, but there is one striking similarity.

Here's what both boys and girls ages thirteen to seventeen had to say when asked what would be their dream job:

### Male Teens' Dream Jobs Ranked in Order

| Professional Athlete | 12 percent |
|---|---|
| YouTuber/Streamer | 11 percent |
| Musician | 6 percent |
| Professional Gamer | 6 percent |
| Doctor or Nurse | 5 percent |

### Female Teens' Dream Jobs Ranked in Order

| Doctor or Nurse | 13 percent |
|---|---|
| Actress | 11 percent |
| Musician | 9 percent |
| Artist | 7 percent |
| YouTuber/Streamer | 6 percent |

Boys are typically encouraged to dream big and unrealistic while young girls are always encouraged to be safe and practical, so it's no surprise the top choice for young girls is to become a doctor or nurse, despite over 57 percent of women physicians leaving their jobs at academic medical institutions versus 32.4 percent of their male counterparts, due to physician burnout.[20]

So what should you do if you are middle-aged and questioning every career decision you've made in life to date? It's time to go back and ask that child in you a question, but you have to ask the right one to get you back to her original desires.

Ask yourself: *What was something you absolutely loved to do as a child?*

This is one of the first questions I often ask my coaching clients and, with good reason, it doesn't matter if they're working with me for life, business, executive, entrepreneurship, or high-performance coaching.

The activities we loved doing as a kid are the closest in alignment to the motivations that will drive us authentically as adults. They are what we loved and found value in prior to absorbing the expectations of everyone else around us, including our parents, friends, teachers, partners, and others.

If I were to answer this question it would include:

- Talking, I was a chatterbox.
- Creating something from nothing in the form of art or music.
- Performing, whether it was music or drama, I loved being onstage.
- Being in nature, especially at the beach with a breeze in my face.
- Curating thrift store finds for my closet or future home.
- Being in constant motion, especially as an athlete.
- Reading and learning anything and everything I could get my hands on.

As we grow and evolve into adults, it's easy to become disconnected from the things that bring us joy because we start placing weight in the thoughts and opinions of those we depend on, as evident in the statistics I shared earlier of millennials' parents influencing their career choices, either consciously or unconsciously.

One of my earliest memories when it comes to money is a perfect example of an unconscious action. I was around eight years old and in the back seat of a car with my father and uncle in the front seat. They were business partners in everything they did, and they'd brought me and my brother along as they opened a new warehouse location. In this situation, we were driving from the airport to the location.

I was being my typical chatterbox Corrie when my uncle turned around and said, "Corrie, I'll give you five dollars if you can be quiet for just five minutes!" Overjoyed, I immediately took him up on that deal. I was motivated! I watched the 1980s digital dashboard clock tick down those five minutes, and the second it was up, I announced, "Time's up! Where's my money?" and held my palm out.

The second my uncle handed me that crisp, new $5 bill, I swelled with pride. I'd *earned* that bill myself. Little did I realize how that experience would affect me into adulthood, not necessarily in good ways. Not only did it sway my decisions in choosing a career path based on my preferred activities, but it also reduced my earning capacity tenfold.

Why is this? Because the main message I internalized was *"When I am quiet, I get paid."* Drilling down further, there were other, unspoken, messages:

- I love talking, but other people don't like it when I do.
- The only time I provide value to others is when I'm quiet.
- My thoughts, ideas, and life experiences are not valuable, so I shouldn't share them.

- It's not worth it to speak up because you'll only be asked to be quiet anyway.

The ironic part about all of this is, as an adult, I've since found my true calling as a professional speaker. It still blows my mind that people actually pay me to talk! And when I do, it's with joy, fulfillment, and ease because it's not only something that comes naturally to me, it's something I've loved doing and excelled at since I was young. For me, needless to say, speaking is a passion.

Getting here, however, was not a pleasure cruise. It's taken me years of inner-child therapy and coaching to unpack all of my fears and recognize that other people's judgments say more about their shortcomings than mine. With much soul-searching and work, I was able to rediscover my passion and purpose. It all starts by getting to know your inner child better and by accepting that there is value in the activities that brought you joy during those formative years.

Circling back to my original question, *"What was something you absolutely loved to do as a child?,"* when you go two to three levels deeper and analyze the root of those activities, it becomes easy to identify things you could be doing professionally, or that could bring you peace and fulfillment (value) in your downtime. You do this by simply asking "why" before each answer.

So, for example:

Q: What was something you absolutely loved to do as a child?
A: Talking

Q: Why did you like talking?
A: Talking allowed me to ask questions and learn about people.

Q: Why did you want to ask questions and learn about people?

A: When I learn about people, it's easier for me to connect with them.

**Q: Why do you want to connect with people?**

A: I want people to feel seen and heard.

**Q: Why is it important for you to make people feel seen and heard?**

A: I know how it feels to not feel seen and heard, and I want to prevent others from ever having to feel that way.

Notice how the last question becomes a core motivator that I now leverage in my career. I now pride myself on helping my clients and audiences feel seen and heard—and I do it all through talking and communication!

Let's unpack another childhood activity that I now leverage in a more personal capacity for fulfillment.

**Q: What was something you absolutely loved to do as a child?**

A: Curate thrift store finds for my closet or future home.

**Q: Why did you enjoy curating thrift store finds?**

A: I love visualizing exactly what I want and finding it at an amazing price.

**Q: Why do you love visualizing exactly what you want and finding it at an amazing price?**

A: Because I can create the exact wardrobe or space I want using the resources I have available.

**Q: Why do you want to create the exact wardrobe or space you want using the resources you have available?**

A: Because I love looking at and wearing objects that bring me joy and are unique, not mass produced, and are environmentally friendly and one of a kind.

Q: Why is it important for you to own and wear objects that bring you joy and are unique, not mass produced, and are environmentally friendly and one of a kind?

A: Because they are one of a kind, and I take pride in being one of a kind as well.

Over the years I've always done everything I ever could to stand out and be one of a kind, including having turquoise hair at one point in my SVP career. It's something I value, and it makes me happy in a way I can't explain.

When you ask yourself the right question, along with the right follow-up questions, it'll lead you to the next step in gaining clarity and determining your personal values, which we'll cover in the next chapter.

But for now, take a beat and use these questions to attempt to reconnect with your inner child and see what the answers say. It may surprise you.

## Putting It All Together

## Getting Off the Wheel

If you've made it this far, you've probably realized that settling doesn't always look like giving up. Sometimes, it looks like achievement, like stability, like a life that's "good enough." And yet, deep down, there's a whisper. A weird feeling you can't quite shake (like mine was). Maybe it's a sense of restlessness, a quiet exhaustion, or a persistent thought that there must be more to life.

We've explored the ways women are conditioned to chase the wrong metrics, to fear disrupting the status quo, to stay small under the weight of good-girl conditioning. We've unpacked how we're taught to measure our worth by external achievements rather than our internal joy.

But awareness is just the first step. Because knowing you're settling and actually doing something about it are two entirely different things. The hardest part isn't admitting that you're unhappy. It is figuring out what to do next. This is where most people get stuck. They hesitate, waiting for clarity, waiting for a road map, waiting for the perfect moment to make a change.

Here's the truth: Change doesn't come from waiting. It comes from a single decision. I know this because I waited, too. I told myself I was happy. I convinced myself I should be grateful. I ignored the unsettling feeling in my gut and even lied to my therapist about it—until I couldn't anymore, until life threw something at me (literally) that made change an easy choice. Because sometimes, the easiest way to make a major change is when you realize you actually have a choice to begin with.

In the next chapter, I'll take you back to the moment everything in my life shifted, to the moment I had to decide, once and for all, whether I was willing to let go of everything I had built in order to step into the unknown.

If you're standing at that precipice right now, unsure of what to do next, this chapter is for you. Because making a major change doesn't have to be terrifying. And sometimes, when you finally take that leap, you realize the safety net was never behind you—it was inside you all along.

# Chapter Three

# The Easy Way to Make a Major Change

*It is in your moments of decision that
your destiny is shaped.*
—Tony Robbins

I honestly don't remember what he threw at me, but I do re-member what he said. And it terrified me so much that it's seared in my memory forever.

It was a morning that started off as any other. The early morning sunlight was streaming through our sheer curtains and reflecting off the mirror I used to put my makeup on. It blinded me as I tried to get my eyeliner just right. I rushed because I was already running late for work, which I absolutely could not afford to be. I was fresh off maternity leave, and the breadwinner for our family; not even the primary breadwinner . . . the *sole* breadwinner.

That's when I heard my five-month-old son *coo* from the other room. It was absolutely adorable, a "Hey, Mama, I just woke up!" sound, which should have made my heart sing. Instead, it made it drop sharply. I was always walking on eggshells and was unsure of what would happen next. I rushed to finish my makeup, patiently waiting for his father to wake up and tend to him so I could get finished and out the door. He was still sleeping off an evening of alcohol, Adderall, Xanax, and Ambien from the night before, so I knew deep down there was a fat chance in hell that would happen.

That's when I suddenly felt something fly past my head, hit the door with a loud bang, and heard him yell, "SHUT THE FUCKING BABY UP!"

Stunned, I stared at myself in the mirror, frozen. A flurry of thoughts swirled through my head: *Do I go in the room and quiet the baby? SHIT! I'm running late for work! Why hasn't this asshole woken up yet? I can't see; this light is blinding my eyes!"*

That's when a thought so terrifying crossed my mind, and it couldn't be ignored: *Wait a second. If he threw that at me, what's to say he won't throw something at our son if I leave him home here with him?*

That really got the thoughts churning: *Should I leave? Should I take the baby with me? Where would we even go? I don't have childcare; I need to work or we'll have nothing. I worked so hard for everything we have here. If I leave, it'll all be gone in an instant; am I ready for that?* I was overwhelmed with complete and total fear of the unknown—paralyzing fear.

The crazy part about this situation is, to this point, I had honestly believed *he* had male postpartum depression. Every day, I'd get home from working a ten-hour day, and there would be an empty six-pack of beer on the table. He'd hand me the baby and walk out the door to head to the bar. So a week prior, I had done research on local therapists. I had given him an ultimatum that he needed to go get help and gave him the numbers covered by our insurance to pick one to make an appointment with. He went to one session, came home, admitted being unfaithful to me throughout my entire pregnancy, and then went on to blame me for it!

The blame game did a number on me mentally, on top of everything else I had going on, so I then called one of the therapists I had researched that he hadn't used: a woman named Elizabeth. I went to have my own session with her to try to piece together how I'd ended up where I ended up. She told me I wouldn't believe her, but I was in an abusive relationship, it was very dangerous, and I needed to take my son and leave immediately. I had been so overwhelmed with day-to-day life, trying to balance my SVP career and being a new mother to an infant, that I had honestly forgotten she had ever said this until the moment he actually threw something at me.

And when he did, suddenly, everything in my life I had been in denial about became crystal clear: I could not, and would not, leave my baby home with him. I realized in that moment that I feared more what would happen should I stay than the unknown of what would happen if I left. It was no longer safe, which made the not-so-easy decision to leave and start my life over that much easier.

## Facing Female Fears

I've learned since then that there are two ways to become motivated to make a major change. There's the "easy" way, which is what we're going to discuss at length in this chapter, and there's also the more common—albeit difficult—way, which we'll discover in the next chapter. We'll get to that later, but because I'm a born-and-bred

New Yorker who only shoots straight talk I'll warn you now: You only want to leverage the difficult way in the absolute, worst-case scenario.

The easy way is by *deciding to make the change* and *doing it on your own volition*, facing your fears head-on, and being afraid but doing it anyway (which is the definition of bravery by the way). It's having a full understanding of how you got to where you are today and deciding that you need to change your actions to receive a different result. As I said, it's the "not-so-easy" easy way.

There's a lot to unpack about fear when it comes to the differences between men and women. In their report "Brave men and timid women? A review of the gender differences in fear and anxiety" Carmen McLean and Emily Anderson present substantial evidence that women not only report greater fear, but are also more likely than men to develop anxiety disorders.[21] This is further supported by a 2023 Gallup Poll, showing that while 40 percent of all Americans fear walking alone at night within a mile of their homes, the degree of fear is much higher in women versus men: 53 percent compared to 26 percent respectively.[22] What are women so afraid of that they refuse to walk alone at night? In a viral 2024 post, over 65,000 women shared they'd feel safer with a bear than they'd feel being with a man.[23] But the truth is our fears aren't directly caused by our proximity to men, especially when it comes to the fears of making major changes. It's far more complex than that and actually rooted in safety and security, as evidenced by the 65,000 women believing bears are a safer option to be left alone with.

## The Fear of Losing Stability

A whopping 29 percent of women participating in my working mother research project cited fear of losing security, especially their jobs, flexible working arrangements, or homes as their deepest, darkest fear. This makes a lot of sense, especially for mothers who are responsible for the safety and stability of not only themselves but their children as well.

Due to this, many women feel paralyzed when faced with big changes because they weigh security versus uncertainty, whether it is leaving a toxic relationship (like me) or job, or stepping into a leadership role and losing their stable schedule. Our fear of loss, whether that is financial security, reputation, relationships, or identity, often outweighs the fear of remaining in unfulfilling or even dangerous situations. This is especially evidenced by my inability to realize I was in an abusive relationship despite my intuition telling me something wasn't right, until it actually became violent. I was so afraid of losing my childcare, and therefore my income and security for me and my son, that I was willing to overlook the fact that my son's childcare provider was intoxicated while caring for him. The question we need to start asking ourselves is *What's the real risk—losing what I have or losing myself—in the process of staying?*

## The Myth of Certainty

Women are often conditioned to wait for certainty before making a decision,  whether it be in their career moves, leadership choices, or personal decisions. From a young age, we're praised for being careful, thoughtful, and responsible while the boys surrounding us are often encouraged to be bold, decisive, and risk-takers. This in itself is an interesting observation, since the top fears cited by adult men range from fear of failure, incompetence, and being perceived as weak,[24] which directly correlate to how they were encouraged to behave as children.

Girls are also taught to consider others' feelings and avoid actions that might create discomfort or disruption, making us more hesitant when making decisions that could cause conflict. This leads to commonly cited issues in the workplace, such as women not applying for jobs unless they are 100 percent qualified.[25] That way, they are certain they'll meet all the criteria and get it.

To further complicate things, women are also often judged far more harshly than men for making imperfect decisions. Society holds us to a higher standard of competence, making us feel like we need to be 100 percent sure before acting. If we make mistakes, we are more likely to face criticism, doubt, or reputation damage. On the flip side, men are often given more leeway to fail and are often praised and encouraged to try again.

Look at the way the media treated Britney Spears following her 2007 mental breakdown versus Charlie Sheen's in 2011. Spears was painted as being mentally unfit to care for herself and others after walking into a salon and shaving her head of all things. In her memoir *The Woman in Me,* she describes the postpartum depression she was experiencing, the grief of losing her aunt, and the stress of her divorce as being the driving motivators to do it. In the aftermath, due to the way the press painted the situation, she lost custody of her children and lived through a thirteen-year conservatorship.[26] She was deemed dangerous to everyone, most of all herself.

Sheen, on the other hand, goes on national TV and later a horrendously overhyped national tour, ranting about "tiger blood," and it results in memes about "#winning!" despite the man behind the scenes being in rehab for addictions, as well as facing charges of assault and domestic abuse. Both celebrities made what were considered lapses in judgment in the moment. However Charlie Sheen's shortcomings and failures were celebrated as funny in the media, his efforts to check into rehab were commended, and his requests for privacy in the media in the years that followed were honored. Little was mentioned of his plea deals, being released, and then continuing his wave of assaults on his ex-wives, as well as even medical technicians, in the years that followed.[27]

Spears lost her self-advocacy and overall identity, and all Sheen lost was his role on a hit TV show. According to the press and society, Spears should have been more careful and considerate in her decisions while Sheen should be celebrated and commended for failing over and over again.

This unequal treatment leads to many women over-rationalizing or waiting for permission to take action. As a result, any intuitive thoughts and feelings we may have surrounding the situation get drowned out by analysis paralysis. As an example, look at how long I stayed with my ex-husband despite coming home every day and seeing he drank a full six-pack while caring for our infant son. I still felt like I needed absolute certainty that it was a dangerous, unsafe situation before knowing that leaving was the right move because, heaven forbid I would have left and he didn't really have a problem and I was overreacting, how was I going to answer those questions when asked of me?

## The "All or Nothing" Trap

Many women often feel that making a big change must happen all at once, which increases fear and resistance. However, major change doesn't have to be one giant leap but can instead be a series of small, intuitive steps that slowly build confidence. To reframe this, instead of seeing leaving a job or relationship as a catastrophic upheaval, how can we reframe it as a series of small, manageable, intuitive decisions that lead to change?

A great example of this is Laura, one of my executive coaching clients. Working as an engineering leader on a mostly male-dominated team, she was ready to quit over constantly being excluded from important meetings she was a stakeholder in. As a new mom to an infant, she feared losing the stability of her income, as well as her flexible work-from-home arrangement, if she just up and quit the same day. She felt stuck in her situation, was unsure of where to start, but had a deep knowing that she was capable of much more.

So instead of making one big change and handing in her resignation, she started making small, manageable changes. First, she started working toward improving her own communication and boundary skills with her existing team, which was terrifying in and of itself. Next, she added searching and applying for her next opportunity and challenging herself to look for roles above her current position. In the process, she not only upleveled her leadership skill set to the tune of gaining the respect of her boss's boss, who previously used to dismiss anything she said, but also maintained her feeling of security in that she didn't feel pressured to take any new job offers for non-remote roles simply because she needed the income to support her family. She had the time and freedom to wait for the right opportunity to come her way, while simultaneously modeling for other women on her team how to lead and gain respect in a toxic work environment.

After a little less than a year of working together and making small, incremental changes in how she was choosing to show up, she shared that she had finally landed a new position. It was a promotion from where she was at with an over 13 percent pay bump that she successfully negotiated in an industry she was passionate about. She was finally going to be able to exit the toxic workplace holding her back, and in the process of doing so she had upleveled her skill set to make her an even more effective leader. She became so effective that it only took her three months working in her new role before she was promoted *again* into an even higher leadership role at her new company.

Her success is proof positive that you don't need an all-or-nothing approach to achieve relief. It's entirely possible to improve and upgrade your situation incrementally as you go.

## External Voices Versus Your Inner Voice

Society, family, and workplaces often send messages that contradict women's inner knowing, making them doubt themselves. We're frequently told we are "too emotional," "overreacting," or "not thinking it through" when we express concerns about a situation.

The best example of this is how women are regularly gaslit when it comes to our own health. One 2023 study shows that middle-aged women with chest pain were twice as likely to be diagnosed with mental illness than their male counterparts.[28] I don't know about you, but I'm not exactly sure how chest pain equals a mental health issue. Yes, we understand we're slowly going insane, but it has more to do with being dismissed every time we advocate for what we know is wrong with our bodies than it does with actually having a mental illness! Oftentimes when we feel something is wrong with our bodies, we're told "it's normal," or "you're just getting old," or "you need to adjust your expectations."

As a result, our intuition is often dismissed because it isn't logical, provable, or validated externally, even though it's often right. Very recently, I had been experiencing a stream of negative health symptoms ranging from extreme hair loss, rapid weight gain (twenty pounds in three months), inability to regulate my temperature, dry skin, brain fog, and crippling fatigue. I'd brought these concerns up with my GP for over three years, including my own research showing how my symptoms mirror an auto-immune condition running three generations in my family. I asked her for a specialist referral, and my GP dismissed and denied it despite there being a more than six-month wait list to see a specialist in my area. I later found a specialist, and while I don't have an autoimmune disorder, I had a slew of other issues that my GP never tested for that were causing all my symptoms. I'm finally feeling better, and it's taken me more than four years to get resolution on something that could have been solved from a simple blood test; all because my doctors felt they knew more than I knew about my own body. Needless to say, I fired them.

If you know deep down that something is wrong, it's important to trust that, no matter what anyone around you might tell you.

## Numbing, Distracting, and Overexplaining

Instead of trusting our intuition, many women cope by overanalyzing and thinking, *If I just do more research, maybe I'll find the perfect answer.* Or they seek endless external validation by polling friends, mentors, or family for advice instead of sourcing it within themselves.

I'm guilty of this myself, and it was a huge reason why it took me so long to leave my abusive relationship. I needed the external validation of my new therapist to even see that there was anything remotely wrong with my relationship, and even with that, after she told me, I still numbed myself out by focusing on working and my day-to-day life instead of dealing directly with the situation at hand. It took something actually getting thrown at me, in addition to the external validation that it's a dangerous situation when that happens, for me to actually put two and two together and know with confidence that it was time to go.

In addition, many women will disassociate from the decision by staying busy, overworking, or avoiding the issue entirely. Fear-based decision-making often leads to cycles of inaction, regret, and stagnation. Of the one hundred women who participated in my research project, the number of women who reported doomscrolling social media in the evenings just to numb out at the end of the day, or signing up for an additional degree or certification they didn't need to delay the transition of looking for a different job, was staggering.

Looking at my situation in hindsight, it's easy to see that along the way my intuition was giving me all the signs I needed to make that important decision. Had I paid attention, I may have even avoided having something thrown at me altogether because I would have left sooner.

Next, let's break down how to trust your own intuition so you'll realize the signs are already there and waiting to guide you too. That way, you can push past your fears and choose to take action from a place of confidence instead of fear.

## How to Trust Your Intuition

I know what you're probably thinking: This is all well and good, Corrie, but how in the hell am I supposed to know if something is a decision worthy of jumping straight into my fears for?

Whatever decision it is you've been putting off, not unlike my own to leave my abusive marriage, I bet you've been ruminating on it for months, if not years, resulting in an endless cycle of analysis paralysis and increasing anxiety.

Here's the telltale sign: If you've been thinking about it, or it's been bothering you for that long, it's more than likely a sign you've been ignoring your intuition.

Intuition is simply a process that allows us to know something without relying on analytical reasoning. It's incredibly important, especially when it comes to leadership. In the report Guts & Gigabytes by the Economist Intelligence Unit, 41 percent of leaders ranked their own intelligence and intuition as the most important factor in their decision-making, followed by 31 percent experience of others and 23 percent data and analytics.[29] That "feeling " enables us to bridge the gap between the conscious and nonconscious parts of our brain. Intuition also helps bridge the gap between instinct and reason.

The primary reason we ignore our intuition is because we've been conditioned to instead trust our ego. Instinct, otherwise referred to as ego, and intuition serve two different purposes.

In the most basic sense: Instinct has everything to do with your survival, safety, and security—all things we've already discussed at length as being of particular concern for women, especially. In our capitalist society, instinct has us believing we need the house with the white picket fence and 2.3 kids and the six-figure salary to be safe, whether it be financially or through the caretaking, approval, and support of others.

Intuition is the complete opposite: It's all about ensuring that the things you do align with your highest good.

I know that the lines can get a little blurry at times, so let me share an example with you: Let's say you're working at a dead-end job, and you're unhappy with it. Your instincts might tell you not to quit simply because it's your safest choice, not unlike what my coaching client Laura thought. After all, that same job helps put food on the table. It provides the flexibility you need to care for your infant. It keeps a roof over your head, and it ultimately helps keep you safe and secure.

On the other hand, your intuition might tell you a completely different story: It might tell you that this job is not the right fit or not challenging enough, the environment is toxic, and that you're better off starting a new career or, maybe, a new business. It might tell you that you'll be happier if you leave and start something new, to proactively and willingly start over from zero.

As you can see, intuition can also be a very powerful tool. But how do you know which one to listen to?

Before diving in and trusting what intuition tells you to do, let's first talk about how you can identify it in the first place. With so many emotions and feelings that we're constantly dealing with in our lives, it's easy to mistake one for the other. So, how do you know it's intuition and not just another emotion?

Here are a few ways you can tell:

## Intuition Is a Strong Gut Feeling That You Can't Just Shake Off

Believe it or not: Your unconscious mind is looking out for you, trying to protect you from danger. So when you feel that intense, nagging feeling from your gut (or chest) that you need to run away from something, it's probably your intuition telling you to take flight. And in most cases the uneasiness won't stop until you heed its warning.

For abuse survivors like me, every time you have the feeling you are walking on eggshells, that's your intuition speaking. Not surprisingly, I haven't had that feeling since I made the decision to leave my abuser.

## You'll Always Feel at Ease After Following Your Gut

No matter how scary a decision becomes, whether it's leaving an abuser like I did, dropping a $20,000 investment in your business, or grabbing a once-in-a-lifetime opportunity, you'll always feel at ease after following your gut.

The day I left my ex-husband, after work I showed up over two hours away on my parents' doorstep with nothing but my baby and whatever I could shove in a suitcase that morning. When I walked into their house, I felt like I literally dropped the weight of the world by placing my suitcase on the floor, symbolically letting go of my baggage from the life I had just left. That feeling of relief was my own intuition validating my choice.

## Intuition Could Come in the Form of Exceptionally Vivid Dreams

When we constantly think of something, our mind subconsciously registers it as essential to our reality. Once it does, that something sometimes comes in the form of dreams. And if it's backed by intuition, that dream could become vivid *and* persistent.

For a very long time, even prior to me making the decision to leave, I had these recurring dreams about airports. In these dreams, I'd always find myself stuck, and I couldn't find my gate. I couldn't get to where I needed to be. Oftentimes when I'd call or text my soon-to-be ex-husband in the dream, the number wouldn't work or he wouldn't answer, keeping me stranded. To say the least, that dream left me feeling uneasy for a while.

After I left I noticed the dreams stopped, so I began to research dream meanings solely out of curiosity. That's when I learned that the airport dream in particular was a manifestation of a very big decision that I had been putting off for a while. To my surprise, once I finally took the leap and made that decision, that particular vivid dream about airports just stopped.

## You Constantly See the Same Opportunities Popping Up Everywhere

Undeniably, this is one of the most common ways that intuition works. It's hard to explain, but when you feel like you see opportunities everywhere, it's probably your intuition trying to tell you that it's safe and time to take the leap.

In my case, I had my parents offer to look after both me and my son postpartum at one point during my maternity leave. My ex-husband had stayed at home. It was like a mini vacation being with them and was in stark contrast to what little support I had from my ex-husband on a daily basis. The week I spent with my parents was filled with some of the best memories I had from my entire maternity leave with my son. I felt safe and cared for in a way I didn't at home. After I left there that week, in the back of my head my intuition knew that was an opportunity for a safe and welcoming space. So when I had to make the split decision after having the object thrown at my head, I knew where I should take my son to be instead, even if it was over two hours away from where I was currently living.

I had also researched therapists covered by my health insurance, not with the purpose of enrolling in therapy myself, but to get my soon-to-be ex-husband to a therapist. So when all hell broke loose and I was looking for answers regarding why my marriage was disintegrating, I already had a list of numbers I could call to find support. I truly believe I intuitively selected Elizabeth first, despite knowing nothing about her, because the Universe had intended her to be that guide for me. Little did I know she's continued to be a guide for me in the almost decade following this event.

The Universe shows you signs of what you should be doing. These signs could come in any form, like a feeling, a book, billboard, or statement shirt, or a person that all seem to point in one direction.

## You'll Have Intense Clarity in Moments of Downtime

I know this is incredibly difficult to imagine, especially if you're a working mother like I am, but imagine being alone in a quiet room. Blissful, right? You have the time to think, daydream, and contemplate. And suddenly, you feel a clarity that is so intense—it's like you're seeing everything for the first time.

I'll never forget one weekend morning a couple of weeks prior to my decision to leave my marriage. I had spent the night at my parents since my soon-to-be ex-husband had admitted his infidelity an evening earlier, so I left to stay at their home to *think*.

My son had woken up in the pack-and-play crib next to my bed, *cooing* not unlike how he did on that fateful morning. I picked him up and placed him in the bed with me. We both lay there, staring at the lights on the ceiling directly above us.

It was in that silence that I heard, clear as day, a voice say, *"Everything is going to be okay."* Just hearing those words released a stream of pent-up tears and allowed a wave of relief to sweep over me.

I like to believe that the voice I heard was my guardian angel. Either way, there's no question that it was through the space and quiet I finally had in the chaos that was my life that my intuition had the opportunity to literally speak up and be heard.

## Your Thoughts Are Often Pulled in a Consistent Direction

As I mentioned before, intuition can become very persistent and nagging, so if you have a thought or idea about something that you previously dismissed, and you often see it coming back again and again, then it's most likely your intuition speaking to you.

Prior to leaving, for a couple of weeks I had a very, very bad feeling every time I got home from work and saw the new empty six-pack of the day on the table. Every time I saw it, I'd imagine a scenario where my son would be in his crib, crying and needing attention but his father was off somewhere else, drinking. The feeling went well beyond my gut and was something I felt deep within my core, but I ignored it. Looking back, I know now this was my intuition speaking to me.

## You Feel and Experience Physical Symptoms

Another way that your intuition could be speaking with you is through physical symptoms. Some people might feel ill. Others might feel the exact opposite: invigorated, inspired, or in the flow.

I was so in the weeds juggling working ten-plus hour days, being up all night nursing my son, and just trying to survive the stress of my life that I didn't have time to even reflect on the physical toll it was taking on me. It only took a week of living at my parents' house for my father to share one morning at breakfast that he thought I looked ten years younger. It still amazes me to this day that I was carrying so much physical stress that to others I looked a full *decade* older than I actually was.

If you're feeling ill or run-down, it's most likely your intuition telling you that it's time to make a change. If you're feeling invigorated or inspired, it's most likely your intuition trying to tell you that you're doing the right thing, and so on.

Now that we've gone through all the ways that intuition can speak to you, let me give you a few tips on increasing your intuition so you can confidently tap into this inner wisdom.

# Easy Ways to Increase and Nurture Your Intuition

At this point, you might be wondering how you can harness the power of your intuition so you too can confidently make easy, "not-so-easy" decisions. Here are five of the easiest ways I've found to increase and nurture this specific skill set.

## Prioritize Your Inner Voice

I know, it can be challenging to tell which voice in your head is your intuition. But if there's one thing you can do to differentiate it from the rest, it's this: Just think back to the first thought you had when faced with that particular decision. Here's the thing: Intuition is usually the very first thought that comes into your mind before your brain kicks into overdrive and your ego starts throwing reasons at you to play it safe.

Your inner voice, the very first thought, is the one that you should listen to and pay attention to.

## Spend More Time in Purposeful Solitude

Believe it or not, emotions, especially negative ones, can cloud your intuition as much as they can cloud your judgment. But you can get past all the noise that's bothering you by giving yourself more alone time. This doesn't mean spending your entire day locked in a room and away from people. In fact, there are tons of different things to help you spend time in solitude productively. Some of my personal favorites are:

### MEDITATION

I like to think of meditation as brain exercise. When you're capable of turning off your thoughts at the drop of a hat, you're also giving yourself some space for self-awareness in your thoughts and actions. Think of it as gym time but for your brain.

## JOURNALING

Journaling is another way to clear your mind and let go of the things bothering you. It's also a great way to get a different perspective on things and gain insight into your own thoughts. Ultimately, it will allow you to be able to function at a higher level of clarity than you could if you aren't getting those thoughts on paper. We'll be talking about journaling more in the next chapter.

## SCHEDULED DOWNTIME

One of the main reasons why women have a hard time trusting their intuition is because they're constantly busy. We're always in a rush and continuously looking for ways to get more done in less time. When we're constantly in this state, it's difficult to feel in alignment with our own intuition, and it's essential to recondition your mind that, as a human being, you can't be on the go nonstop. You need a little breather every once in a while too.

Scheduled, purposeful downtime will allow you the space you need to feel in alignment with your intuition, be immersed in your own thoughts, and not just be pressured into another person's agenda outside of that downtime.

Don't get me wrong. Your downtime doesn't have to be fancy. You can go for a walk in nature or do a hobby you love. The bottom line is to just move away from other people's thoughts, beliefs, and ideas for some time so that you can give space for yours. When you do, you allow yourself both space and time to listen to your inner voice.

## Take Cues from Your Body

If you'd like to be more in tune with your intuition, you'll also need to learn how to listen to your body. These tiny signals, like your body's cues and all forms of physical sensations, can help you understand your gut feelings better.

For example, if you feel ill in the presence of a certain person, then something must be out of alignment. It could be that your inner voice is trying to tell you something about that person. Either way, don't just dismiss these sensations as a figment of your imagination.

The bottom line is to pay attention to your body. If you do, you'll learn to trust your intuition a whole lot more.

## Look Up the Meanings of Your Dreams

Dreams can tell us so much about ourselves. But more often than not, we have no idea what they mean. If you want to gain a deeper understanding of yourself and your intuition, you might need to explore the meaning of your dreams, especially those that are recurring. You can do this by reading a few articles online, asking ChatGPT to analyze your dream, or even checking out dream books so you can have better clarity on what those dreams mean for you and be able to address any issues that may be bothering you.

## Learn the Art of Detachment

Without a doubt, we all get emotional. And it's completely normal to feel negative emotions like anger, frustration, sadness, and disappointment. But especially as a leader, whether it be in our households, communities, or workplace, you don't want to make emotional decisions. They come from a place of your ego speaking and are rarely done with the highest good for all involved.

Let me stress this point once again: You need to make decisions from a place of clarity, even when you're feeling a whirlwind of emotions. How? The first step is for you to take a beat and identify those emotions for yourself. Ask questions: *How am I feeling? Am I feeling sad, upset, angry?* Then really sit in that feeling and decipher what it's trying to tell you. Usually once it's acknowledged, it's easier to identify the root cause and you can then easily detach from it and move on.

Once you've done that, make an effort to push that particular thought to the side, even temporarily, to make some space for clarity and allow you to decide what to do next. Whenever you feel wrong about something, give this exercise a try, and I'm sure you'll be amazed at how incredible it is.

Please note that I'm not saying to ignore your emotions completely. They will always be a part of your life. But what you can do is understand that you can detach from them temporarily so you can make effective and clear decisions. Doing so will help you become more connected to your intuition in the long run.

## Putting It All Together

# Making a Major Change (the Easy Way)

By now, you understand that making a major change is rarely easy, but there are two distinct ways it can happen.

This first, which we've discussed at length in this chapter, which I call the "easy" way (though let's be real, it's not that easy), is when you recognize the signs, trust your intuition, and make a conscious decision to change before the situation forces your hand. This is the path of self-awareness, proactive courage, and choosing discomfort in the short term to build a life that actually aligns with your values.

In this chapter, we've unpacked:

- **Why women experience fear differently than men** and how societal conditioning impacts our decision-making

- **The biggest fear-based roadblocks that keep women stuck,** including the fear of losing stability, the myth of certainty, and the all-or-nothing trap
- **How intuition is our greatest asset in decision-making** and how to tell the difference between fear-based instincts and true inner knowing
- **Practical ways to strengthen and trust your intuition** so that when a major decision arises, you don't hesitate, you move

If you've been waiting for a sign, this is it: The time to make a change is before you no longer have the luxury of choosing it. But what happens when life doesn't give you that chance? What happens when a moment comes that you didn't see coming—one that rips the foundation out from under you and forces a transformation—whether you're ready or not?

That's what we're about to explore next.

If this last chapter was about learning how to choose change, the next is about what happens when change chooses you. And trust me: There is no easy way through it.

Let's talk about the second, more difficult way to make a major change—the kind that comes when the unimaginable happens—and you're left picking up the pieces of a life you never planned for.

# Chapter Four

# The Difficult Way to Make a Major Change

*There is nothing permanent, except change.*
—Heraclitus

My heart was beating so fast, I thought it was going to pound right through my chest, and it had been going at this rate for close to two hours.

I see the exit of my post-divorce, long-term boyfriend, Franco, up ahead and for a second I am relieved I don't have farther to go. It's the last Friday in June during peak New York City rush hour, and the Hamptons summer traffic started in full force, slowing what would have been a forty-five-minute drive from Brooklyn to Long Island to a snail's crawl.

I've been stuck in bumper-to-bumper traffic for the entire time. From the moment I sat in my office, staring at my cell phone after

I placed it back on my desk, following the call I made to Franco's office and learning he'd never reported to work that day. Every single morning without fail, from the day we started dating until the morning prior, he texted me good morning. I knew something was wrong when that expected message never arrived. The call to his boss later this morning confirmed it.

I finally pulled up to his apartment, and my heart sank the second I saw the police cars, though I was not surprised to see them. I had called 911 to request a well-being check once I was stuck on the highway and knew it was going to take me a while to get there. I had been talking to the police the entire way since they had to call me to get the code to enter the building. Thank God his apartment had digital keypads and I knew the codes by heart.

As I ran from the car and into the building, my heart did not skip a beat, continuing to pound . . . pound . . . pound . . . and the world around me went silent. I didn't hear the sirens. I didn't hear my footsteps. I seemed to float up the stairs in slow motion to his second-floor apartment, where I was stopped by two police officers at the top of the stairs.

"Where is he? Where's Franco!" I exclaim, my words sounding as if they were being said underwater. I was completely out of breath and my heartbeat was now pounding out of my ears.

"I'm sorry, ma'am, we can't let you in there," one of the officers said as he gently started escorting me back down the stairs and out the door.

*"Is he okay? Why not? What's going on?"* I scream and try to claw my way back up the stairs.

That's when he tells me, "I'm so sorry ma'am, but Franco has passed."

I scream, but I don't hear it. All I hear is a tinnitus ring. It's like I'm screaming into a void in excruciating pain and no one can hear me.

At this point I am sobbing and hysterical. The news does not compute. Last night, we had made plans to go to a concert at this exact time today. A couple days prior, we had gone to a movie, and I had spent the night here in his apartment while my son was at his grandparents. Last week, we had discussed getting engaged, and him moving into my house, and last weekend we had taken his two boys, both only one to three years older than my own, and my son to Dave and Busters, and the kids all had a blast. They were best friends, you can't ask for more when attempting to blend families. We had even discussed expanding our family further, on vacation together a couple of weeks prior, when he suggested starting to try for a baby together.

We had made life plans *together*. This was not a part of those plans. Therefore, *this can't be real.*

"If he's passed, why can't I go in and see him?" My voice was now raw as I pleaded through my tears.

The officer had finally managed to maneuver me outside the apartment building, and we were standing on the paved walkway. I could feel the hot June sun beating on me and burning me alive on the pavement. I thought to myself, *This is what hell on earth must feel like.* That's when the officer shared news I never, ever expected to hear.

"He didn't die of natural causes."

At first this news didn't make sense. It took a couple of minutes for me to fully process the gravity of that statement and for me to understand what it meant.

"Is there someone you can call to come and wait with you?" the officer asked.

He paused for a moment, and with hesitation continued, "Unfortunately, we can't allow you to leave the scene just yet. The detectives are on their way."

He paused again to gauge my reaction, which was still shock, and then continued, "Since you were the one who initiated the well-being check, they need to speak to you first to rule you out as a suspect of any foul play."

Talk about adding a new layer of trauma to the already most traumatic experience of my life. I took a breath and responded under my tears that I could call my mom, which I did. Luckily my parents only live fifteen minutes away from Franco and both had an idea something was up. I had to ask my dad for permission to leave work early to find out what was going on.

The officer who was with me at that point was assigned to watch me while the rest continued the investigation in the apartment and we all waited for the detectives. I was pacing back and forth on the grass trying to process the reality of the situation in front of me. I called my therapist, Elizabeth, who thank goodness I had just started working with again a few weeks earlier to figure out why I was feeling *weird*. I shared with her what had happened, and all I remember her telling me was "Don't worry, you'll get through this, and you won't be alone. We'll do it together," while I stared dead-eyed into an overgrown boxwood bush outside the apartment building's window.

After hanging up the phone, my arm dropped limply by my side. I stopped pacing and gazed upward, looking toward the sun. It was around 5:30 PM and the sun was still high in the sky and as powerful as ever after hitting the summer solstice a couple of days earlier. The sunlight blinded me, so I closed my eyes. I could feel its warmth making me sweat in the 90 percent humidity and my warm tears mixed with that hot sweat as it dripped down my face and off my chin. That's when a surprising thought, almost as if sent from the heavens above, crossed my mind. *"Corrie, you've been through worse in recent years. You'll get through this. This is a fact."*

For the first time in close to three hours, my heart stopped pounding, and I felt a sense of peace wash over me. Then a sudden burst of clarity hit me like a perfectly executed right hook. I thought, *Corrie, everything you knew in life to be true this morning now isn't. Life can change in an instant. STOP MISSING OUT ON YOUR LIFE!*

I decided right then and there, on that lawn in the blistering hot June sun, that if this was a third chance at starting over to lead the life of my dreams, then I was going to do it my own way for a change.

## There's Before, and There's After

There are moments in life that divide everything into before and after, moments that arrive uninvited, that shatter your sense of certainty, that rewrite your entire reality in an instant. This is the difficult way to make a major change, and no one gets to opt out. Sometimes it's a job loss, a diagnosis, a betrayal, a death, a moment that gut-punches you into a new reality you never asked for and weren't ready for. These are the kind of moments that force you to see that whatever version of life you were clinging to no longer exists.

That day on the lawn, outside Franco's apartment, blistered by the June heat and immobilized by shock, I remember feeling like the world had dropped out from under me. But I also remember something else, something I didn't share with anyone at the time. A thought came through, sharp and clear, cutting through the grief like a crack of light: *You've done this before, not this exact kind of loss, but the feeling, the trauma, the total collapse of everything you thought you knew.*

I remembered what I had already been through—the abuse, the divorce, the sleepless nights as a single mom trying to hold a career and a life together with shaking hands—and I realized: That was the training ground.

As wild as it sounds, I knew on that very day—before I even had time to fully process what had happened—that I had already learned how to survive this. I had done so well surviving events like this that I had my therapist suggesting I completely change careers to help people do the exact same thing, not unlike what Tony Robbins does.

More than that, I knew right then and there I wanted to understand how. I wanted to know what exactly had allowed me to keep going through all of it without completely losing myself, without burning everything down, without sacrificing my performance, my purpose, or my ability to love again.

So, I did what I've always done in the face of overwhelm: *I analyzed it*. I picked it apart, piece by piece, and I looked for the patterns. I studied the questions I kept asking, the habits I returned to, the thoughts that healed me, and the ones that didn't. And what I found was that there were five core patterns of thinking, reacting, and coping that consistently showed up, not just for me, but in every overwhelmed woman I've talked to or coached.

These are what I now call the Overwhelm Culprits. This chapter was the turning point that led me to define them. In the chapters that follow, I'll walk you through each one. But before we dive into the framework itself, you need to understand this: If you've ever found yourself facing a life-altering moment, the kind that rips the rug out from under you and dares you to figure out who you are now, you are not alone.

Recognizing this experience is crucial. By identifying and addressing the underlying factors that contribute to overwhelm during such pivotal life transitions, we can better equip ourselves to navigate them. This understanding led me to develop the Overwhelm Culprit framework, which we'll explore in the following chapters to provide strategies for managing life's inevitable challenges. And while I would never wish those moments on anyone, I want you to know that they don't have to be the end. They can be the beginning. My own was my third opportunity in life to start over again.

But it's not enough to just get through it. You deserve a way to move forward with clarity. With intention. With the tools to not just survive but to choose your next chapter on purpose and do so on your own terms.

Let's start by understanding what's been keeping you stuck—and how to change it.

## Introducing the Overwhelm Culprits

It's strange the way clarity sometimes arrives, not with fanfare, not with full answers, but with a quiet knowing that something has to shift and that you're the only one who can do something about it.

That day on the lawn, still sweating in the unforgiving sun, I realized life wasn't going to wait for me to be ready. It wasn't going to pause until I had a perfect plan. It was going to keep coming, and I had a choice: I could keep surviving, or I could learn how to actually live through the chaos. In that moment, I made a decision. Not just to survive what had happened, but to pay attention to how I had survived the last time. After my divorce, I hadn't just rebuilt my life; I had done it without crumbling professionally or personally. I had grieved, yes. But I had also grown. Somehow I had managed to maintain my career, care for my son, show up for others, and eventually, find love again.

So I asked myself: *What allowed me to do that?*

What tools did I already have that helped me hold it all, even when everything was falling apart? And could I use them again now?

I didn't know it at the time, but those questions would become the starting point for the framework I now call the Overwhelm Culprits, five hidden but powerful root causes that fuel burnout, disconnection, stagnation, and emotional exhaustion in high-performing women like us.

I wasn't looking for a branding hook. I was looking for a lifeline. I took out a notebook and wrote down every single thing I did after my divorce that had helped me feel stronger, steadier, or more like myself. Patterns emerged. I grouped them, then regrouped them. I tested them in real time while walking through the depths of suicide loss, and what I found was this: Whenever I felt overwhelmed, stuck, lost, or unsure, it almost always traced back to a breakdown in one of these five areas:

1. Lack of Clarity
2. Lack of Confidence
3. Lack of Community
4. Lack of Conditioning
5. Lack of Consistency

That's five culprits—all of them fixable—five root causes that quietly, but consistently, keep high-performing women stuck, stalled, or spiraling. You might be doing everything right on the outside, but if you don't address what's really driving your overwhelm underneath the surface, progress will always feel just out of reach.

Each culprit creates its own unique roadblock. And until you name it, you can't change it. Here's a high-level look at all five:

## Lack of Clarity

This isn't just about knowing what you want—it's about understanding why you want it. Without that deeper sense of purpose and alignment, it's easy to spend your time taking action . . . in the wrong direction. Or worse, to stop taking action altogether because nothing feels meaningful enough to pursue.

## Lack of Confidence

Let's say you do know what you want. Great! But if you don't believe you're worthy of having it, or capable of making it happen, you'll self-sabotage before you ever start. Doubt is one of the most powerful forms of resistance. And it doesn't always shout. Sometimes, it whispers so quietly you don't even realize you're being held back.

## Lack of Community

You might be crystal clear on your goals, and fully confident in your ability to reach them, but what if you're surrounded by people who can't see the same vision or who actively doubt your growth because it challenges their own? You'll stay stuck. We become the average of the people we spend the most time with. Choose wisely.

## Lack of Conditioning

When I say conditioning, I'm talking about both mental and physical health. It doesn't matter how ambitious you are, if your body is exhausted, your mind is running on fumes, and you're constantly pouring from an empty cup, there's no bandwidth left to create meaningful change. Self-abandonment might look noble on the surface, but it will cost you everything over time.

## Lack of Consistency

Growth doesn't come from grand, one-time gestures. It comes from small, often boring actions repeated over time. The right systems, boundaries, and habits are what separate momentum from mediocrity. If you don't have structures in place to support your progress, you'll keep starting over every time life gets hard, and that cycle alone will wear you down.

Each of these culprits may show up at different times in your life. Sometimes they overlap. Sometimes one is so loud it drowns out the rest. But there's good news. Once you understand which one is running the show, you can start to take back control. That's what this book is about. Not just identifying which culprit is sabotaging your growth, but giving you the practical, strategic tools to do something about it. These chapters are designed to help you get honest about what's holding you back—not in a judgmental "I should be further along" kind of way, but with the compassionate lens of a woman who has been there. Multiple times.

## Putting It All Together

## The Difficult Way to Change

You didn't choose the storm, but you do get to choose who you become in the aftermath.

If you're reading this book, chances are you've already had your "lawn moment." Maybe more than one, the kind of moment that splits your life in two, into before and after. Maybe you're in the thick of it right now, or maybe you're still trying to make sense of a version of you that no longer fits the life you're living. No matter how you got here, you're not broken. You're not behind. You're not failing. You're overwhelmed, and likely for good reason. But that ends here.

This chapter was the turning point for me, and maybe it will be for you too. This was the moment I stopped letting life happen to me and started learning how to respond to it with intention. That starts by understanding what's driving your overwhelm, naming it clearly, and then choosing how you want to move through it.

The framework I've introduced here, the Overwhelm Culprits, is meant to give you that clarity. And while I'll walk you through each one in the coming chapters, I've also created a tool that can help you identify where to begin.

It's a free quiz that helps you discover your personal Overwhelm Culprit. If you're eager to understand which one is most active in your life right now, or if you're struggling to figure out your next step, it can give you a starting point. You can take the quiz at www .corrielo.com/overwhelmculprit.

That said, I still encourage you to read the entire book, in order. Even if one culprit stands out more than the rest, the truth is they all connect, and by understanding the full picture, you'll be better equipped to create real, lasting change.

So, let's begin at the root.

We start with the most foundational culprit of all: lack of clarity, and how reconnecting to your internal GPS can help you reclaim your power, your purpose, and your next step forward.

# Part Three

# The Five Overwhelm Culprits

# Chapter Five

# Lack of Clarity: Your GPS to Success

*If you have no destination, you'll never get there.*
—Harvey MacKay

As I sat immobilized in traffic, the GPS estimated time of arrival didn't budge. It was as if time had stopped altogether and I was stuck in between two different realities instead of idling in the same spot on the Belt Parkway for the past thirty minutes.

Ever since I had moved into my new house in March of that year, I basically lived in my SUV. After living with my parents for six months and scraping together every dollar I had, I eventually found a home I loved and could afford only forty-five minutes from the city and halfway between my job and my parents. As an added bonus, it was ten minutes from the beach. However, the commute was absolutely brutal.

Every morning, I would wake up an hour before my son would wake up to leave for work, and I wouldn't get home until maybe an hour before he went to bed each evening. Honestly, the most I ever got to see him was through my home's security camera systems when I would check in on him during my lunch breaks while he'd play with our au pair. Yet I never put two and two together that living that way shouldn't feel normal, because when I looked around me I saw validation of my circumstances:

**Everyone lived their lives like this.** Look at all these people stuck in traffic going to work with me. Who was I to be special and have anything different?

**I had everything I had always wanted.** A beautiful new house, a child, an amazing career, even the white picket fence; I was living my definition of success, as I shared in Chapter 2.

**I had made commitments to others I couldn't break.** If I did, I'd fail to live up to everyone's expectations and disappoint so many people that I cared about.

What most people don't know about me is I actually don't have a business degree. I have a super expensive piece of paper that says I can draw well—a fine arts degree. After I graduated, I had no job prospects and found myself waiting tables to pay the bills (super cliché, I know). This frustrated my father, who had helped contribute to the expensive piece of paper, and as a solution he suggested I come and join the family business as a graphic designer. When I agreed, I vividly remember him telling me: "You're sure this is what you want to do? Because when you're in, you're in for the long haul. You're committed to the family business."

Back in 2003 when he made the invitation, I had figured I'd spend a couple of years there, figure out what was next, and move on to the next thing. What I didn't anticipate was I'd seemingly blink, it would be fifteen years later, and I'd be running the entire operation as an SVP. Here I was an art school student and former waitress who made her way to the top of running a large, regional operation with no formal business training or degree. I couldn't just walk away from that; I had already invested too much in it. I also honestly loved working with my family. I was committed to them, as well as to my career progression and one day taking the company over when my father decided to retire. I would daydream about passing it down to my son one day, so I dealt with the shitty commute.

My commute didn't only take a toll on me mentally in that I never got to see my kid; it also took a major chunk out of my finances. It was *insanely expensive.* One day, I decided to add up the total number of hours I spent on the Belt Parkway commuting while I paid my au pair to take care of my son. Want to take a stab at how long it was? How about *twenty hours* a week. I was literally paying my au pair a part-time salary, just so I could commute to my full-time job. It was excruciating to not only be away from my child for that long but also to have so much money and dead, unproductive downtime wasted away each week simply driving back and forth to work. There were more mornings than I could count that, once I'd get into the office, I'd have to shut myself in the bathroom, have a good cry, and then head to my desk and start the day.

What I've learned since then is you'll never get to your destination if you don't have an exact address to program your personal GPS (your internal Goal Positioning System) to create routes to take you to your goal. A personal GPS will always find multiple different ways to get there and will reroute you if you get stuck for a bit like I often did on the Belt Parkway. But if you don't know exactly where you're going, just like that phone app, it's going to route you in circles until you finally make a decision on exactly where to go.

I was definitely driving in circles. Despite feeling overwhelmed by never seeing my kid, suffering a horrendous commute, and the pressure to not fail my family, I willingly stayed in that cycle because I believed I had everything I wanted: the career, the kid, the beautiful suburban house. I was clear on the previous destination, I'd arrived after all, but I wasn't clear on where I was going next, or why I even wanted everything I've ever wanted, until I experienced the suicide loss.

I didn't know it then, but my Overwhelm Culprit was *Lack of Clarity.*

I never would have been able to figure out the why, as well as what step to take next, had I not understood, evaluated, and done three years earlier what I'm about to share with you in this chapter.

## Time to Unstuck Yourself

In coaching, there are three questions that need to be answered in order to get someone past whatever is keeping them stuck and not taking action. They are:

1. Where are you today?
2. Where do you want to be?
3. What's getting in the way?

The reason people hire coaches to help them get unstuck is because it's incredibly rare to have the self-awareness necessary to answer these three questions accurately.

In a series of surveys, organizational psychologist Tasha Eurich found that 95 percent of people think they're self-aware, but only 10 to 15 percent truly are.[30] When asked, how does one become more self-aware, she points out two aspects to address: internal and external self-awareness.

Internal self-awareness involves looking inward and doing the work to fully understand your passions, values, and aspirations. External self-awareness involves understanding how people outside yourself see you.

We're going to cover more on external self-awareness in the next chapter. For now, let's take a deep dive together into really understanding yourself from the inside-out, and answering the questions of where you are today, where you want to be, and what's getting in your way. But first, it's important to understand how and why you became stuck to begin with.

## Too Many Choices, No Clear Direction

Sometimes, the problem isn't lack of goals—it's too many competing priorities pulling you in different directions. The mental load of juggling career, family, relationships, and self-care makes it impossible to see the big picture.

Take research participant Nicole, a working mom juggling a household filled with kids, pets, and a busy spouse alongside her career as a pharmacy technician at a hospital. With the hospital constantly running 24/7, and her kids having a demanding sports schedule, she shared frustration in that she feels pulled in too many different directions with no clear solution to reign it all in. There are never enough hours in the day to devote to her making the moves necessary to advance in her career, never mind taking some time for self-care, which was necessary since she's expecting her next child. This resulted in her constantly being on the lookout for time management and productivity hacks, including a giant family shared message board and calendar that she has difficulty getting everyone to use regularly.

Without clarity, every decision feels exhausting, and staying in place feels easier. When your personal GPS feels like you are standing at an intersection with a hundred roads in front of you, but you have no idea which one to take, you do what feels easiest—you'll simply stay where you are.

When you have a tool that allows you to take a snapshot of where you are at the intersection of all those forks in the road today, it becomes so much easier to know which one to venture down. I'll share with you one of my favorites in one of the following sections.

## The Pressure to Meet Other People's Expectations

Many women subconsciously build their goals around what's expected of them—not what they truly want. That or they allow other people's expectations to start to cloud and disconnect them from what they originally wanted, like I did.

Take research participant Alyssa from Chapter 2, a working mom and mother of two, ages four and one. A healthcare professional, she was highly accomplished in her field, especially overseeing starting a new heart surgery program. Her core frustration she shared during our conversation was how she felt like she was being crushed under the pressure and expectations everyone had of her, both at work and at home.

Despite all her accomplishments, she still feared judgment anytime she wanted to step outside the traditional narrative of success of medical providers in her field. Working on a male-dominated team, she felt like she was constantly being judged for every decision she made, and she worried that if she set better work-life boundaries, her colleagues would view her as a slacker. Her need for external validation was so strong that when it came time to negotiate her contract, as much as she wanted to negotiate for higher pay, she didn't feel like she "deserved" it and found herself looking for permission to do so. In a conversation she shared she had with her husband regarding the negotiations, she said he answered, "And this is why men make more money than women" much to her disappointment. Her frustrations and belief that she's not meeting everyone's standards keep her from making the bold choices that would actually make her happy. I know exactly how she feels, because I was once in the same position she was in.

There were so many expectations set on me as the third generation heading my family's business. As time went on, it became very difficult for me to envision what I wanted for myself without first thinking of how it would affect both my family and the business. It was a stress I carried with me each and every day. I endured that commute and then sat in the bathroom bawling my eyes out when I finally got to the office. If I was late, even if I couldn't help it due to the traffic, I always felt like I was being judged and that I'd failed everyone.

I've since learned one of the best ways for reconnecting with your sense of self, and reigniting those dreams and desires, is by tapping into why you even journeyed on this path to begin with. In my case the reasons for my career choices had changed, but I was unaware of it. This caused me to feel incredibly unfulfilled, in addition to being stressed in my current position. I'll be sharing with you shortly an incredibly simple method I walk all my coaching clients through to discover their own why, and their corresponding purpose.

# You're Already a Success

"I have everything I wanted, so why do I feel stuck?" I'm not the only one who's felt this way. Many high-achieving women check all the right boxes—career, family, home—but still feel unfulfilled or lost due in large part to having already achieved everything they had aspired to do.

Remember my executive coaching client Laura from Chapter 3? She initially enrolled in coaching because despite having reached the top of both her professional goals (leading an engineering team) and personal goals (starting a family), she had zero idea of what was next for her after she had achieved both. Having a baby was an enormous life change, which had her feeling like she'd lost her identity in the process as well. This led to her feeling an overall discontent in her role because it no longer felt challenging for her. She had figured it would be harder to balance motherhood and her career than it was, and the situation made her realize she was falling short of her true potential.

It's also common to feel guilty for even admitting dissatisfaction when everyone on the outside looking in sees what you have accomplished and assumes you're happy. That or worse, you are expected to be working toward something by those close to you that you don't really feel inspired to pursue.

When it comes to feeling unfulfilled in your life and career, it really comes down to one thing: You've become disconnected from why you had chosen this path to begin with.

# The Cycle of Busyness and Autopilot Decision-Making

Many women stay stuck in the cycle of daily survival, never pausing to ask: "Am I even going where I want to go?" In short, is your personal GPS correctly set?

Take Lisa, a research participant, law firm partner, and forty-four-year-old mother of two young children, ages two and six. She shared with me that maintaining her current pace was  unsustainable, but she'd been so wrapped up in a day-to-day routine and momentum that it provided zero breathing room to consider anything else. That said, she was unsure how to even begin making a change, never mind how to know if she's actually headed in the life and career directions she wanted.

Lisa feared that if she didn't do something soon, there would be serious health implications. With her identity being so closely tied to the success she had already achieved in her career, she found herself putting off major decisions or changes surrounding a possible career change and instead kept searching for solutions to help her manage both more efficiently.

The next logical step for Lisa is to question if this is the lifestyle she even wants to continue in this new stage of her life. Does it align with where she actually wants to be five years from today? She was making choices based on momentum, not intention.

In order to know if it's the direction you want to be heading, you need to have clarity on your destination. Here's how I had gotten clarity on my own.

## *Exercise*

# To Cure the Lack of Clarity Overwhelm Culprit

Having suffered the effects of the Lack of Clarity Overwhelm Culprit myself, I've spent hundreds of hours and thousands of dollars searching for ways to gain more clarity. I've tried everything from working with therapists and coaches, taking online courses, reading books. You name it, I've tried it!

In this section you'll find all of the exact exercises I once used to cure the culprit for myself. They worked so well they later became the foundation of the frameworks I've utilized in my coaching practice since starting it in 2018.

All the exercises are laid out according to the three key questions mentioned earlier: Where are you today, where do you want to be, and what's getting in the way?

Take a moment to write down your answers. Feel free to do them directly in this book, or if you'd like a worksheet, you can visit www.corrielo.com/overwhelmculprits-resources to download a copy.

## Balancing Your Wheel Using the Wheel of Life

When it comes to ways to help you figure out where you are in the current moment, one of the very best exercises I've ever encountered for that is a traditional life coaching exercise called the Wheel of Life.

The premise is simple. You draw a circle and divide it into eight sections, each representing an area of your life you have a stake in. Categories can include:

1. Friends and Family
2. Health
3. Significant Other
4. Personal Growth
5. Fun and Leisure
6. Home Environment
7. Career
8. Money

Each line drawn represents a spoke on the wheel of life. Closest to the center ranks at a 0 while closest to the outer edge of the wheel ranks at a 10.

On a scale of 0–10, rate each area of your life with zero being sorely needing attention and 10 being happy as is, no change necessary.

When completed, your wheel will be lopsided in areas. These are the urgent priorities, the areas you need to bring immediate attention to in order to balance your life and get the wheel spinning again.

This exercise gives you a very clear visual representation of where you are today, even if you don't necessarily have clarity on how you ended up here. To understand that, you need to work with a mental health professional. Therapy helps you gain clarity in understanding your past so you can identify repeating patterns and not make the same mistakes over and over again. Coaching helps you gain clarity on what you desire in the future and identify the action steps needed to get there.

# Discover Your Why

I will never forget the first day I was introduced to leadership expert Simon Sinek's work. It had been about one year since my divorce, and things were finally settling down for me. I had taken my then eighteen-month-old son on a cross-country trip I affectionately called the "friends and family" tour, where we visited four states, flew between two coasts, and saw around twenty of my nearest and dearest friends and family over the course of seven days. I know, insane with a toddler, but totally worth it!

Since I had been spending so much time commuting at home, I had an overflow of various audiobooks on my iPhone to comb through. At the time, I was trying to ramp up my leadership skills so I could show up more effectively for my team. I had popped Sinek's *Start with Why* on the sound system while I drove up the coast of California from San Diego to Los Angeles. I remember listening to him describe his concept of the Golden Circle while driving and overlooking the Pacific Ocean, and it resonated so deeply that it became a core memory for me. It's like he turned a switch on in my brain, and I have never been the same since.

That single book, as well as its corresponding TED Talk,[31] later became part of the foundation of how I now coach women in both personal and professional development because it shows how by communicating from the inside out—from why you do what you do to how and what you do—it resonates with the masses on a deep level. The vast majority of both individuals as well as organizations are not clear on their why, and it often shows through their marketing.

The following is my adapted version of Simon Sinek's Golden Circle, tailored to how I work with overwhelmed, high-performing women leaders.

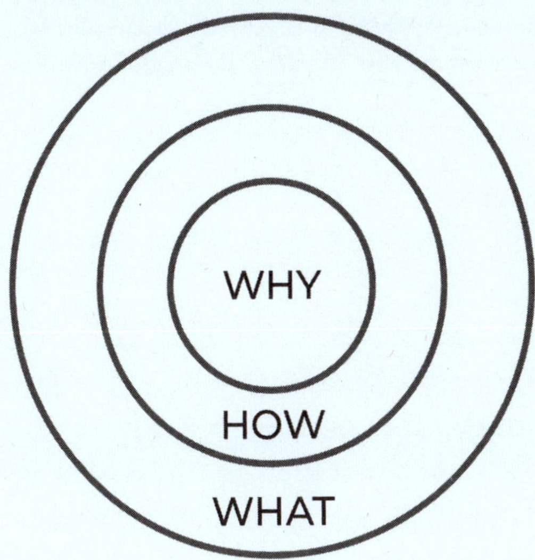


Let's break down the rings of the circle and the clarity you gain by answering the questions.

## Why

At the center, the core of the circle, is *why*. This asks the question, *Why do you do what you do*? It's about your purpose, the causes important to you, and your beliefs. The majority of individuals, as well as organizations, cannot answer this question.

## How

*How* breaks down how you do it. In business terms, this is your unique selling proposition (or USP). It's what makes you different from everyone else.

## What

*What* answers the question of what you do. This is the question most people can answer, and they never bother to go the two steps deeper into the center of the circle.

Let's break down a couple of examples I've used in the past to help demonstrate how this works. I'll provide examples from an organization as well as an individual (myself, at the time I learned this method).

- Warby Parker

  Why: to lead the way for socially conscious businesses

  How: a revolutionary price

  What: designer eyewear

- Corrie LoGiudice (circa 2016)

  Why: to help families start family businesses

  How: out of the box, creative marketing to compete with big-box stores—*thank you, expensive piece of paper!*

  What: senior vice president of sales, marketing, and operations

Back in 2016, I was passionate about helping families start local businesses. It was part of the work my own family's business did in wholesale distribution. Small mom-and-pop shops would sign up with us to represent the Fortune 500 electronics brands we distributed, and my team was responsible for teaching them everything they needed to know to market, sell, and operate their businesses.

The part I love most about Sinek's Golden Circle exercise is that it makes it ridiculously easy to create mission statements. Here's a breakdown of a typical mission statement followed by Warby Parker's so you can see how they align in comparison to their Golden Circle.

## YOUR MISSION STATEMENT

Why you do what you do, how you are different, and what you deliver to fulfill your mission to others.

### WARBY PARKER:

To offer designer eye wear at a revolutionary price, while leading the way for socially conscious businesses.

Mission statements can be incredibly valuable for organizations but more so for individuals. Your mission statement can stand in as your North Star, helping guide your decisions and intentions alongside your personal values. We'll be covering values in the next exercise.

From here, I highly recommend checking out Sinek's TED Talk (URL is included in the Endnotes) and mapping out your own Golden Circle. When you do, it's important to remember one important thing: Your why can change at any given moment.

This is where I had originally gone wrong when it came to my horrendous commute. But more on that shortly.

## Reconnecting with Your Values

Back in 2018, after I'd quit my safe, secure, fifteen-year career and considered jumping off the deck of a cruise ship, I had the idea of wanting to start a business as opposed to finding another job. So I hired a life and business coach named Shannon Kaiser to help me figure out what the hell I should be offering. I remember, like it was yesterday, her asking me, "What are your personal values?" and drawing a blank. As someone who always prided myself in being incredibly self-aware, it was a tough pill to swallow.

The problem was, I knew what my personal values *used* to be. I had always assumed you live by certain values and they stick with you for life! But that's not how personal values work. They change and evolve as you grow and evolve as an individual. I had done a *lot* of growing and changing in a very short five-year time span, which is why I was drawing a blank. Living my life on a day-to-day basis had made everything intolerable. I had to start over with new values because I had started my life over.

To figure it out, I needed to pick new values to represent how I wanted to live my new life moving forward. As a self-professed perfectionist, I toiled over each and every value so as not to make the egregious error of selecting the wrong ones—a practice I do *not* recommend.

Instead, all you have to do is review the following list of 105 personal value options  and pay attention to your intuition, using the methods you learned in Chapter 3. Select your top four, and if you doubt your intuition's selection, you can always use the coaching question framework I shared in Chapter 2 to ask yourself "why" until you get to the core resonating factor. When you look at the value and it resonates in a way you can't explain, you know you have the right one.

## LIST OF 105 COMMON PERSONAL VALUES

| | | |
|---|---|---|
| Achievement | Contribution | Financial Stability |
| Adventure | Confidence | Forgiveness |
| Ambition | Connection | Freedom |
| Authenticity | Creativity | Friendship |
| Accountability | Curiosity | Fun |
| Balance | Determination | Generosity |
| Belonging | Dignity | Grace |
| Beauty | Diversity | Gratitude |
| Boldness | Efficiency | Growth |
| Career | Empathy | Happiness |
| Compassion | Excellence | Harmony |
| Collaboration | Equality | Health |
| Commitment | Fairness | Home |
| Community | Faith | Honesty |
| Competency | Family | Humility |

| | | |
|---|---|---|
| Humor | Optimism | Simplicity |
| Inclusion | Parenting | Spirituality |
| Independence | Passion | Stability |
| Innovation | Patience | Success |
| Integrity | Peace | Sustainability |
| Intelligence | Perseverance | Teamwork |
| Intuition | Personal | Time |
| Joy | Development | Tradition |
| Job Security | Playfulness | Travel |
| Justice | Professionalism | Trust |
| Kindness | Recognition | Truth |
| Knowledge | Reliability | Understanding |
| Leadership | Resilience | Uniqueness |
| Legacy | Respect | Usefulness |
| Learning | Responsibility | Vision |
| Love | Resourcefulness | Vulnerability |
| Loyalty | Security | Wealth |
| Mindfulness | Self-discipline | Well-being |
| Nature | Self-expression | Vitality |
| Open-mindedness | Self-respect | Wisdom |
| | Service | |

When I did this exercise, my top four values were *family, health, career,* and *travel.* After claiming them as my own, it made decisions so much easier both personally and professionally without subconsciously conforming to other people's expectations. For example:

- A team member requested to take some personal time to see their child's school play. It was an easy *yes* since I value family and they do too.

- A friend asked me to go out dancing with her on a Thursday night. Doing so would prevent me from waking up on time to get my workout in. So that decision would be misaligned with my value of health, so it was an easy *no*.
- An opportunity popped up to do some professional development in an area I've always wanted to master. It was an easy *yes* since it was aligned with my career value.

You get the idea, and this isn't even the fun part. Once you have your four values selected, you can jump into creating a future life vision that aligns with and complements your personal values and tackle the aspiration portion of internal self-awareness. More on that next.

## Your Five-Year Vision

Did you know that only 3 percent of the population sets goals? And of those who set goals, only 1 percent actually write those goals down. This is important because writing them down makes you 42 percent more likely to achieve them. Making them time bound and sending progress reports to peers increases the chance of success another 40 percent.[32]

Having clear, measurable goals goes far beyond setting SMART (Specific, Measurable, Actionable, Relevant, Time Bound) ones. Having clear, measurable goals also means being able to mentally picture your success and what your definition would look like, especially in relation to your personal values. As a leader, having clear values in business is essential. It informs every area, from how you market to how you hire to how you operate your organization. If you work for an organization that doesn't align with your personal values, there will *always* be some sort of conflict.

Back during my hellacious commute, I had been passing my twenty hours a week in the car by listening to whatever educational information I could get my hands on. I listened to podcasts on healing from narcissistic abuse, audiobooks on leadership, and a lot of entrepreneurship podcasts, including *The GaryVee Audio Experience*. Gary Vaynerchuk (aka Gary Vee) is a fellow New Yorker who at one point decided to leave his family's wine business to start his own and documented the entire journey online. Ever since I came across an episode where he shared his experience, it was like a seed was planted in my brain that perhaps I could do something different than my family's business too.

One morning I flipped past Gary's podcast on iTunes and then out of the corner of my eye caught another show called *Smart Passive Income* by Pat Flynn. Pat's an online business expert who created an online course helping architects study for the LEED licensing exam and saw tremendous success after being laid off in 2008. The thought of being able to potentially make money passively in my sleep and possibly eliminate this horrendous commute and spend more time with my son was super appealing to me. So, I queued up the episode and listened as the traffic finally started flowing again.

In the episode, he plugged a book of his called *Will It Fly?* which covers how to test and validate business ideas. As soon as I pulled into the office parking lot, I added it to my Audible account, figuring it would make for a great listen for my 120-minute ride home later that evening.

As I was listening to Pat narrate the book on my ride home that night, he shared an incredibly simple visualization exercise. It got my brain swirling for the entire rest of the ride, and I couldn't wait to get home, do my dinner and bedtime routine with my son, and finally take an hour to myself to give it a try.

Pat Flynn's "Airport Test" was based on a hiring framework used at Keller Williams Realty. I've since adapted it for the purpose of leadership clarity and personal vision.

Now that you have your top four personal values, creating your own Five-Year Vision is easy.

1. Take a single sheet of 8.5 x 11-inch paper

2. Fold it into quadrants and open it back up.

3. At the top of each quadrant, write one of your top four personal values. When you're done, it'll look something like this:

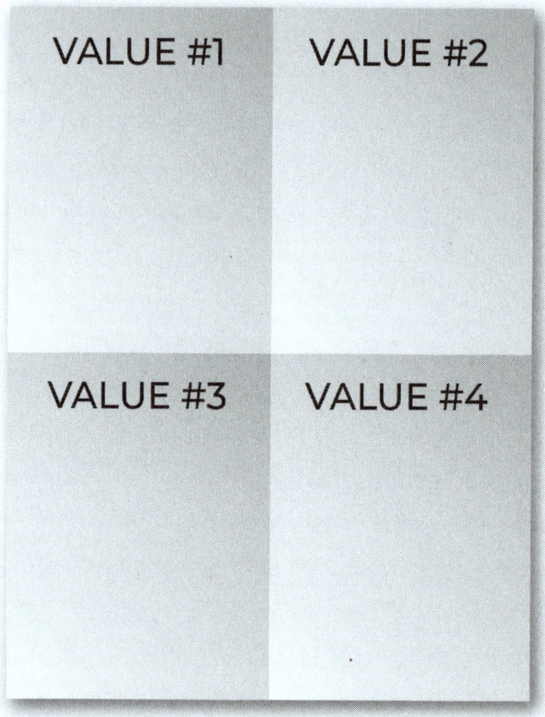


Next, imagine the following scenario: It's five years from today and you're at an airport. You run into an old friend, family member,

or colleague you haven't seen in that timeframe who asks you, "Hey, great to see you! What have you been up to all these years?"

Take the next thirty minutes or so and brainstorm what has happened with regard to each of your four values and the highlights of what you would have accomplished.

Don't censor yourself and use bullet points if you prefer. There's no right or wrong way to do this; the most important thing is that you take the time to visualize what that future success looks like, and be as specific as possible.

I promise you this: Five years from today, you'll refer back to this sheet of paper and be *amazed* at how much of what you visualized is now your current reality. I do this process every five years and it becomes my personal GPS to set my daily, weekly, monthly, quarterly, and annual goals. We'll be covering more on how to do that in Chapter 9. In the meantime, it's important to note what all these exercises set you up to realize next. And that's *why you even want these things* to begin with.

## Having a Goal Is Great, but Having a *Why* Makes You Unstoppable

The night I created my first Five-Year Vision, I folded the paper in quadrants and wrote my four top values. I then set a timer for five minutes, closed my eyes, and started to daydream.

*It's five years from today. I'm at the airport and I run into a family member, friend, or colleague I haven't seen in forever. Okay, let's pretend that it's Gia.*

Gia is a friend of mine from college who's been living in China for several years, so it makes sense I wouldn't have seen her in five years, and if I did, it would be at an airport. I then continued with the daydream.

*Gia asks me, "Oh, wow, Corrie! How are you? What have you been up to?" To which I answer . . .* my thoughts trailed off for a second as I opened my eyes to look at the first quadrant, which said *Family.*

*"Things have been amazing, Gia!"* I imagined myself rubbing a pregnant belly saying, *"I recently got remarried. My son also has two siblings, and there's a third on the way!"*

I paused and thought: *Fat chance in hell of that happening, Corrie! Seriously, you're newly divorced with a fourteen-month-old. Who the hell goes from one kid to four in five years when you're unmarried? Ah, whatever!*

I wrote down the answer anyway, plus a few other bullet points as I brainstormed what my life looks like in five years when it comes to my family.

I looked at the second quadrant, *Career,* and closed my eyes. *"And my career couldn't be more rewarding. I implemented remote work for our team, have added new and exciting products to my family's business portfolio, and am traveling the world as I do it."* I winced, *Corrie, that's never, ever going to happen! You run an electronics distribution operation and literally get paid to move boxes between locations. You can't run that remotely! What's wrong with you?* Once again, I paused and wrote it down anyway.

I took a few more minutes to finish out the *Home* quadrant, including all of the amazing renovations I was planning for the new house, and then wrapped up writing that I'd be a competitive salsa dancer in the *Health* column (because why not?), before I hear the loud beeping of my phone timer telling me that time was up.

Then I clipped the sheet of paper to my office message board, finished the rest of my wine in a giant gulp, turned off the lights, went to bed, and honestly forgot about it. I had no idea the clarity the exercise would give me until a year later when I experienced the worst day of my life.

As I stood on the lawn of my post-divorce partner's apartment, staring at the sun in 95-degree heat, my hot tears mixing with my sweat streaming down my face as I waited for the detectives to arrive to rule me out as a suspect in his death, one thing became crystal clear: Everything I knew and believed to be true that morning was no longer a reality. It also became clear that anyone I knew and loved could be gone in an instant.

I vividly remember thinking of that piece of paper on my bulletin board while I was waiting, and realizing I had it wrong all along.

Family is one of my personal values, so it made perfect sense why I was so dedicated and valued working in my family's business so highly for all those years. I knew by working in the family business, I'd have more freedom and flexibility to be with my loved ones than at another corporate job. It was an added bonus that I got to spend time *with my family*. It was why I was so motivated to become a leader there, and potentially one day pass it down to my own kids.

Where I went wrong was by spending all my time with my family in the family business, and by taking on a twenty-hour-a-week commute to do so, I was missing out on time with the newest member of my family, my son. I was living my life in misalignment with my new vision of success for my family as well as my career.

This realization was a turning point for me, because after having lost my partner, I decided right then and there that I no longer was willing to miss out on time with my son. The next step became clear because I finally *understood* why I was working toward everything I had worked toward. I also understood *what was getting in the way* of that vision. In order to achieve that life, I needed to step down from the family business. My vision of adding products and services to the family business, being able to travel the world, and working remotely and spending more time with my son in the process simply needed to be accomplished by me branching out on my own, instead of staying there.

The next personal GPS destination was set. Now I just needed to trust the GPS would continue to route me through the rest of life's detours, twists, and turns, and set me up for success when it came to bridging the gaps for achieving that vision.

That's the beauty of the exercises I've shared with you today. Each one of them plays a part in putting together the pieces of your clarity puzzle. Once the puzzle is complete, it's up to you to then evaluate what you discovered, look for common themes, and determine what will be necessary moving forward to make your vision a reality.

## Putting It All Together

## Calibrating Your Personal GPS

The Lack of Clarity Overwhelm Culprit is one of the most common reasons we stay stuck. Curing inaction requires developing internal self-awareness as well as clarity on where you are today, where you want to be, and what's getting in your way.

By now you've learned how to gain clarity and internal self-awareness on a scale that only 3 percent of people even bother to attempt. You've also learned how easy it is to feel stuck when:

- You have too many choices with no clear direction.
- You feel pressure to meet other people's expectations and can no longer connect to your own.
- You've already seen success and have yet to decide what's of value to you next.

- You're so busy that you're making decisions from a place of momentum on autopilot.

You've also learned the most effective exercises to help you gain clarity based on the answers to the three key coaching questions.

Where are you are today?

- The Wheel of Life

- Discover Your Why

- Identifying Your Current Core Personal Values

Where do you want to be?

- Your Five-Year Vision

What's getting in the way?

- Putting It All Together

By doing this work, you should also have some ideas about why you want what you want as well as what's standing in the way of your getting it. You have answers to all three questions and have exactly what you need to move forward.

I know what you're probably thinking: *Corrie, this is all well and good. I have a clear idea of what I want and why I want it, but I'm not so sure I believe I can do it (or have it). What do I do next?*

In the next chapter, I'll introduce you to the second Overwhelm Culprit, Lack of Confidence, and give you a clear-cut strategy to bridge your confidence gap and make your Five-Year Vision a reality.

# Chapter Six

# Lack of Confidence: Breaking You Down and Building You Back Up

*Sometimes people try to expose what's wrong with you,*
*because they can't handle what's right about you.*

—Unknown

Close to 183,000 people packed into the Las Vegas Convention Center, where the frigid air conditioning was in stark contrast to the sweltering desert heat outside.

I was there too, over seven months pregnant, and wandering the massive halls of the mega Consumer Electronics Show, otherwise known in the industry as CES. It's the most important business event of my year, never mind the largest trade show in the entire United States. It's also famously male-dominated, such a well-known fact that the publication *Information Age* had just reported on the all-male lineup of keynote speakers that year, as well as the broader issues of gender inequity in the industry.[33] Yet here I was, right in the middle of it all, waddling around the show floor like a penguin and standing out like a sore thumb.

I had feared my pregnancy would make me miss the show for the first time in my eight years of attendance, but at the very last minute my midwife gave me the green light to attend. I was super excited and relieved. Overall, I was feeling energized, even that late into my third trimester. I also was also feeling pretty good about how I looked, having done myself up for the eight hours of back-to-back meetings I had scheduled for the day. I had on the perfect, most comfortable professional maternity shift dress, stylish pointed toe flats, a slick blazer, and I even did my makeup! I never wore makeup aside from the occasional cat-eye liner and mascara, but that day I decided my outfit warranted it. I put on a full face and was feeling myself. All in all, I was confident and ready to take the show by storm, kick ass, and take names while having a blast doing it.

I spotted the huge CES welcome sign and the lineup of tourists waiting to snap their selfies, and thought to myself that I wanted one of my own. What better way to remember my excitement of being there, as well as to document my pregnancy career adventures? After waiting about ten minutes to reach the front of the line, it was finally my turn. So, I positioned myself and snapped a quick pic.

Just as I saved it to my photo album, I remembered that I'd never let my husband know I'd arrived at the show safely that morning. So, I popped the selfie in a text message and sent it off to him with the message "Good morning from CES! How are you doing this morning?"

I continued on my way to the first meeting of my day and made the long trek across two to three football-length exhibit halls to arrive at the first brand booth to meet up. That's when I faintly felt my phone vibrate because I received a return message from my husband. It was so loud in the exhibit hall, I could hardly hear the ring. I checked it while struggling to avoid walking into anyone, and when I read the message my heart sank: "Why are you wearing that lipstick? You look ridiculous. Maybe try taking it off before your meetings, okay?"

This is why I never wore makeup. I had been so preconditioned over the course of our fifteen-year relationship to his comments critiquing my appearance that the ridiculousness of his statement didn't even sink in. Instead, I was immediately mortified, instantly anxious, and completely and utterly freaked out. I now rushed through the crowd as fast as a seven-month pregnant woman could shuffle, struggling to make my way to the nearest bathroom. Every step of the way I checked my watch for fear that I'd be late to my meeting.

I looked in the mirror, horrified that the reflection I had been so proud and excited to capture forever in the selfie in front of the CES sign was now in the bathroom mirror staring back at me. How was this even the same person? I was so confused, the thoughts started swirling and filling up my brain with negativity: *I was feeling like I looked amazing this morning! How could I have been so off?*

I took a giant wad of paper towels from the side of the sink and furiously tried to scrub it off. The red lipstick had stained my lips and wasn't going anywhere, and all the rubbing was making them even redder than they were before.

*"Shiiiiiit! I look like a clown, and there's 183,000 people here to witness it!"*

Still pregnant, still vulnerable, I left the bathroom and forced myself back into the crowd. Where earlier I had felt like an unrecognizable grain of sand flowing among the waves of people, I now started growing increasingly anxious. Everyone's eyes were suddenly on me, judging me as I passed. And there were thousands of them!

When I finally made it to my booth five minutes late for the meeting, my team could sense something was off and asked me if everything was okay. I lied. "Nah, I'm all good. Just took me a bit longer to get here." I tapped my round belly, adding, "Little dude's been dancing on my bladder, I had to make a quick bathroom stop. I appreciate your patience while waiting for me."

We made it to the first conference room, but I didn't take in any of it. All I could focus on was wondering what they all were thinking of me and my *ridiculous* lipstick. People asked me questions and naturally looked at me for a response, but I felt like they were staring at my hideous makeup. I was completely spaced out, in a fog. My fears, doubts, and imposter syndrome raged all at once and drowned out all the other noise, weighing me down through that meeting and the seven after it. It was as if all my titles, accomplishments, and reputation that I had built for myself in that space were immediately stripped from me, and I suddenly no longer belonged in the room because I was so worried everyone thought I didn't look the part anymore.

I didn't know it then, but during this period right before my son's birth and shortly after, following my divorce, my Overwhelm Culprit was *Lack of Confidence*.

I never would have been able to find the courage to leave my ex and start standing up for what my son and I both deserved less than seven months later had I not understood, evaluated, and done what I'm about to share with you in this chapter.

# When Doubt Becomes Your Default Setting

Confidence isn't about never facing criticism; it's about trusting your worth even when you do. But many of us weren't taught this. Instead, we learned to perform for acceptance, to downplay our ambitions to make others comfortable, and to internalize critiques until they became our truths.

We began to believe the voices that told us we were too much—or not enough; that our successes were mere luck; that our ambitions were arrogance; and that our appearances, our tones, our leadership styles were all wrong. So, we adjusted. We toned down our instincts, edited our brilliance, and in doing so, started to doubt our inherent power.

This erosion of confidence doesn't always manifest as overt insecurity. It often appears in our silence, our second-guessing, the opportunities we don't pursue, and the boundaries we fail to set. It's demonstrated in how we tolerate behaviors that chip away at our spirit and in how we misinterpret others' discomfort with our power as evidence of our own flaws.

Here are some of the many ways that the seed of doubt gets planted. It's far more common than you may think.

# Lack of Representation in Leadership

It's hard to be what you can't see. When leadership is overwhelmingly white, male, and childless, or when bold women are labeled "difficult" or "pushy," many women begin to question if confidence is safe or even desirable. They don't lack the *ability* to lead. They lack evidence that they'll be accepted when they do.

It's hard to imagine yourself at the top when no one who looks like you, leads like you, or has the same lifestyle challenges as you is already there. Whether you're the only woman in the boardroom, the youngest leader on the team, the only working mom in a sea of childless executives, or the first person in your family to hold a leadership title, that absence of representation doesn't just feel isolating—it undermines your confidence at the root.

Out of eighty-four research participants, forty-six women—over 54 percent—were unable to name *even one person* who regularly talks about the issues we discussed. These included topics like career growth, motherhood, burnout, boundaries, or confidence. Some left the answer blank. Others explicitly said, "None." Many paused in the moment, searching their brains for someone, and came up empty.

That silence says a lot.

When over half of high-performing women can't name a single relatable figure speaking publicly about what they're going through, we have a visibility problem. It's hard to be what you can't see. And it's even harder to build confidence in a world that doesn't show you enough women who lead with it.

According to a McKinsey and LeanIn.org 2023 report, *only one in four* C-suite leaders are women, and *only one in twenty* are women of color. So it's not a surprise that many women subconsciously believe power is meant for someone else, someone louder, older, whiter, childless, more corporate, less . . . them.

This belief often lives under the surface. It doesn't always shout. Sometimes it just whispers: *"Maybe I'm not ready yet." "Maybe I don't belong here." "Maybe I should just stay where I'm comfortable." "Maybe I shouldn't rock the boat and risk losing my flexibility."*

But here's the thing: Representation doesn't just matter because it's fair. It matters because it expands what we believe is *possible.*

Confidence grows when we see someone who reflects our experience thriving in a space we want to occupy, and when that's missing, we have to build that belief from scratch.

That's not easy, but it's possible. And that's what this chapter is all about.

# Internalized Criticism Becomes Identity

Many women don't struggle with confidence because they lack competence. They struggle because they've internalized years, sometimes decades, of subtle (and not-so-subtle) criticism and mistaken it for truth. We've been told to quiet down, not take up too much space, smile more, stop being bossy, or tone it down. And over time, those messages don't just hurt, they start to stick.

In my own life, I spent over fifteen years in an emotionally abusive relationship where savage little comments slowly chipped away at my sense of self. Some comments I was used to hearing on a regular basis included:

- Your energy is too masculine.
- You're too bossy after business trips.
- Your acne is ruining your face.
- You're not successful, you're lucky.
- You do a terrible job cleaning the dishes (from the man who never did dishes).
- You need to wax your neck, it's too hairy.
- You're a terrible pet parent and will be an even worse parent (before we had kids).

Even at seven months pregnant at CES, an industry event I had attended for over eight years, I still had no idea how deep that conditioning ran. As I've expressed, I had been feeling powerful that day: I was styled in a sleek maternity dress, my hair and makeup were done, and I was energized and excited to take the show floor.

Then, one text from my partner: "Why are you wearing that lipstick? You look ridiculous" was all it took. Two sentences unraveled every ounce of confidence I had built that morning. I sprinted to the bathroom, panicked, and scrubbed my lipstick off with paper towels until my lips were raw. I had walked into that conference feeling like a leader. I left the bathroom questioning if I even belonged there.

That's the thing about self-doubt. It's rarely yours to begin with. You absorb it from people who feel threatened by your light; from environments that don't know how to hold space for your ambition; from family members, teachers, partners, or bosses who confuse control with care. Eventually, you don't need anyone else to put you down, you've learned to do it yourself.

Take research participant Brittany. A driven marketing executive and mother of three, she shared that while growing up, she was often told she was "too opinionated" or "too much." So, she learned to edit herself. She's gotten so good at shrinking that now, even when she's praised at work, she brushes it off, and she knows she does it. She doesn't believe it. It's like she doesn't trust her own voice anymore. She's not alone.

In my research, more than a third of women I've interviewed said they actively question whether they deserve their roles, despite being highly qualified. They defer praise, avoid the spotlight, and second-guess decisions long after they've made them. They're stuck not because they don't know what to do but because they've learned to doubt themselves at every step.

And this doubt isn't always loud. Sometimes, it's subtle. Sometimes, it sounds like:

- "I probably shouldn't speak up in this meeting, it's not my place to."
- "They're more experienced than I am."
- "Maybe I'm not ready yet."

- "I don't want to be seen as difficult."

Self-doubt becomes part of your identity, not because it's true, but because it's familiar.

Where in your life have you mistaken someone else's judgment as your truth? Here's what I want you to remember: Just because someone once told you who you *were*, doesn't mean that's who you have to continue being.

But it's not just about what you internalize from others. It's also about how you respond when you're challenged or corrected.

## Feedback Feels Like Failure

Confidence doesn't just vanish in dramatic moments. Sometimes, it erodes in quiet, consistent ways, like how we receive feedback.

Many high-achieving women are praised for being "driven," "diligent," and "detail oriented." But underneath that drive is often a deep fear of disappointing others. That fear turns feedback, something meant to support growth, into a perceived personal attack. If you were raised in a culture where excellence is the bare minimum and mistakes are unacceptable, it's easy to associate feedback with failure. Not as something to improve—but as proof you're not enough.

In the article "Overlooked Leadership Potential: The Preference for Leadership Potential in Job Candidates Who Are Men vs. Women," an experiment proved how women in leadership were judged more on their performance while their male peers were judged more on their potential.[34] Women are more likely to be questioned, interrupted, and asked to "justify" their decisions in ways men are not,[35] causing women, especially those in male-dominated industries, to feel like they have to work twice as hard to be seen equally as competent.[36]

Take research participant Ella, a single, working mom in a middle management role aspiring to make her way into upper leadership at her organization. She cited ongoing challenges in communication, feeling as if she had to go over and above to explain how as a single head of household she has other priorities she needs to consider that are not optional. The result of those conversations had her constantly on the defensive and being asked to justify her decisions. This had her feeling like every piece of feedback she received was as if she was failing both at work and at home. When I asked what she felt could be a helpful resource to navigate her challenges, she said: "Recommendations on how to respond professionally, even when responding to negative feedback" and how to better handle being put in that situation altogether.

In work environments where women are held to higher standards but given less room to fail, feedback becomes loaded. Instead of being received as a tool for refinement, it lands like a judgment. And that generates constant self-monitoring that creates overwhelm, not because the expectations are necessarily unfair, but because they feel like one more thing you're not doing "right."

We're going to talk more in this chapter about how to rewrite those feedback scripts. But first, it starts with recognizing that feedback is not failure—it's an invitation to grow, not a verdict on your worth.

## Perfectionism Disguised as Professionalism

Confidence isn't always loud. Sometimes it hides behind polished presentations, color-coded calendars, and obsessively edited emails. It's perfectionism and, for a lot of high-achieving women, it's been cleverly rebranded as "professionalism."

We're praised for being prepared, for being thorough, for sweating the small stuff, and never missing a detail. And because the workplace rewards performance over well-being, it's easy to confuse our perfectionist tendencies with ambition. But underneath that drive to "get it right" is often something much deeper, fear: fear of being exposed, fear of being called out, fear of being seen as anything less than capable.

Research participant Jessica, a marketing executive and mom of two, shared how this played out in her day-to-day. She cited the mental load women carry alongside the expectations by society to do everything, not only well, but perfectly, as being her biggest source of anxiety. But here's the truth: Perfectionism isn't protection. It's a societal trap, and Jessica was self-aware enough to know this is not an expectation she wants to pass on to her children, but it's difficult not to with the unbalanced mental load often placed on women.

Jessica said, "I think we put too much pressure on women and girls by default because it trickles down. We have this picture-perfect vision. You're the great wife and you show up at work and have your makeup done and do all these things. It's definitely something very top of mind for me to have my daughter see that it's okay to struggle. It's okay to say you don't have it all together and try to do the best to make yourself the best you can be." She also shared a vivid analogy of what it's like to be a working mother in today's world: "It's like you have a bunch of balls in the air, but you don't drop the glass ones. Rubber ones will bounce back. Our kids are like glass balls. I don't want to drop things with them."

This level of perfectionism convinces you that confidence is something you can earn if you just do everything perfectly. But the bar keeps moving, and the second you slip and drop a glass ball, you question your entire worth.

This pattern isn't rare. A 2020 study by KPMG found that 75 percent of high-performing women have experienced imposter syndrome at some point in their careers, and many cite perfectionism as one of the root causes.[37] Another study by the American Psychological Association links perfectionist tendencies with chronic stress, burnout, and anxiety—particularly among women in leadership roles.

While it may seem like the pressure is coming from the outside (and let's be real, it often is), we're the ones who internalize it. We hold ourselves to impossible standards, then punish ourselves for not meeting them—all while pretending everything is fine. But what if professionalism didn't mean perfection? What if confidence didn't require constant proof? What if the way to be taken seriously wasn't about being flawless—but about being real?

We'll get there, but next, let's break down some easy strategies you can implement, starting today, to rebuild your confidence from the ground up.

## Redefining Confidence on Your Own Terms

Here's the harsh truth when it comes to confidence: It's an inside job. No one else can build it for you. It's not a talent you're born with; it's a skill you build and rebuild over time. It's not a feeling you wait for; it's a decision you make, often in the absence of certainty.

But before you can build confidence, you have to first define it for yourself. Too many women operate under a version of confidence that was shaped by someone else's standards:

- Be assertive . . . but not aggressive.
- Be ambitious . . . but not too ambitious.
- Be visible . . . but not disruptive.

This leads women to constantly chase validation. The problem is they're seeking this validation externally instead of internally, within themselves.

It's no wonder so many high-performing women feel disconnected from the idea of confidence altogether. When the models available to you are conditional at best and punishing at worst, you learn not to trust your instincts—you learn to second-guess them.

That's why the first step to rebuilding confidence is not about trying harder. It's about starting over; this time, on your own terms.

## Conducting Your Confidence Audit

Before we can rebuild, we must first understand where the cracks have formed. The Confidence Audit is a simple but revealing exercise to begin this process.

Ask yourself:

1. Where in my life do I already feel confident?
2. Where do I notice self-doubt creeping in? Where am I allowing other people's perceptions—or my assumptions about their perceptions—to define how I see myself?
3. What actions can I start taking today to bridge the gap?

Do not rush these questions. Do not judge your answers. This exercise is not about fixing anything. It's about observing. Awareness, not action, is the first catalyst for change.

Back when I first did this exercise, the area where I felt the most self-aware was my appearance. I had recently given birth and was still carrying extra weight. After fifteen years of being critiqued on my appearance, I also believed it to be true. So in thinking of the one action I could take to bridge the gap, it was clear as day. I booked myself an appointment at Sephora for a makeover. This was a small but impactful decision that pushed my comfort zone because I was a self-professed "I don't wear a lot of makeup" girl. Either way, after the makeup artist worked her magic on me that day, I left the store feeling incredible about the version of myself who now looked back at me in the mirror. That, plus I left the store with no less than six new lipstick shades I could rock with no one around to criticize me for wearing them anymore.

In my work with coaching clients, this simple audit often reveals patterns that have been operating in the background for years without notice:

- Areas of strength that have gone uncelebrated
- Areas of vulnerability that have been misinterpreted as failure
- Areas of resilience that deserve to be honored rather than hidden

The goal of this audit is not to create a to-do list. It is to create a mirror, one that reflects the truth, not the distortions others have handed you.

## Building Confidence Through Repetition

It might sound counterintuitive, but the only way to truly build up your confidence is to keep doing the things you don't feel confident about until you finally feel confident doing them. This requires repeated actions that often start off as being incredibly uncomfortable because they push your comfort zones but later, through the repetition, become easier on your nervous system to hold space for. The repeated actions also make us more proficient at whatever the task at hand is, meaning that the more we do it, the more and more confident we get.

Once you have visibility about where your confidence currently stands, the next step is to intentionally cultivate it through deliberate practice.

A great example of this is what happened immediately following my Sephora makeover. While I felt I looked good in the mirror, I was still extremely self-conscious that my new lipsticks didn't look as good on me as I thought they did when I came out of the store. I was basically still reliving the trauma of my CES lipstick experience. So, while I wore them every day, I still needed external validation from others.

What followed is a phase that my friends lovingly referred to as "Corrie's Summer of Selfies." I took so many selfies while sitting in traffic on the Belt Parkway, wearing my awesome array of new lipsticks, that it's hilariously embarrassing for me to admit it now. I was still needing the likes and comments on my pictures to validate that I did in fact look as good as I felt. In my coaching, I often refer to these behaviors as Confidence Reps—small, strategic actions taken consistently, not just occasionally, to reinforce the identity of a confident leader.

These actions may seem almost inconsequential in isolation, not unlike wearing a bright-colored lipstick in public:

- Accepting a compliment without minimizing it
- Speaking up once during a meeting when you would normally stay silent
- Setting a boundary around your time or energy without overexplaining
- Advocating for yourself when an opportunity arises, even if your voice shakes
- Not apologizing when you ask for something

But just like building physical strength, emotional resilience is formed through accumulation: one rep at a time, one conversation at a time, one self-trust exercise at a time.

# Sustaining Confidence with Intentional Tools

In addition to building new behaviors, it is essential to create systems that support the ongoing maintenance of confidence—especially when external validation is scarce or old patterns threaten to resurface.

Some of the most effective tools for maintaining confidence that I have used personally and with my clients include:

- Compliments Files
- Personal Affirmations
- Celebration Rituals
- Visualization Practices

These tools are not about bypassing hard feelings or pretending everything is fine. They are about building emotional infrastructure strong enough to weather those moments without losing your footing.

Let's break these down one by one so you know how to get the best bang for your buck out of them.

## Compliments Files

Compliments files are exactly what they sound like. It's a file that can be held on your phone, on your computer, or even in a filing cabinet that holds all the amazing things people have said about you over the years.

I kicked my own Compliments File off following an exercise given to me by a former mentor. She challenged me to reach out to ten to fifteen of my closest friends, family members, and colleagues—people I trusted—to ask them one simple question: "What do *you* think my greatest strength is?" It's important you reach out to no less than ten people, ideally more, because you want to ensure you have a good data set for analysis later. If you don't have a minimum of ten people you can think of to ask this, pay attention in the next chapter because Lack of Community may be your true Overwhelm Culprit and not Lack of Confidence.

When working with my coaching clients, one of the favorite tactics we use to analyze their results is to include all the unedited answers in a spreadsheet and feed it to ChatGPT for unbiased analysis. AI has the ability to spot trends and read data without the influence of my client's own biases about themselves and their own abilities. The results are always incredibly eye-opening—and confidence boosting!

Other things to collect to go in your Compliments File can include screenshots from social media posts with comments, emails singing your praises, newspaper and media features, customer testimonials, and even performance reviews. If someone, *anyone*, has something amazing to say about you, collect that shit so you have it to refer to on a day when you're doubting yourself!

The responses I've received over the years have greatly influenced the work I am doing today. My circle of friends, family, and fellow professionals shared that I was their go-to problem solver, a great communicator, and one of their favorite storytellers. Each and every response I received makes my heart sing, and I still occasionally look at them when I'm having a down day. At this point, my team and I have collected over one thousand post-event audience surveys, and it's growing every day. Any time after a speaking engagement when I worry my message didn't land with the audience, the post-event surveys always have the true answers. It makes it much, much easier to stomach one negative comment when I have hundreds of other positive ones.

## Personal Affirmations

If you're unfamiliar with the term *affirmations*, they're grounded, specific statements that reinforce your agency and value. They are not generic mantras. They are rooted in the reality you are choosing to claim.

According to the National Institutes of Health, self-affirmation activates brain systems associated with processing and reward and is reinforced by future orientation.[38] Repeating to yourself who you are, who you want to be, and what you are capable of—even if you don't believe it just yet—reinforces your subconscious belief of it in the future.

# How to Create Personalized Affirmations (with a Little Help)

Affirmations only work if they feel like they belong to you. The more specific and emotionally resonant they are, the more powerful they become.

I get it: Sometimes it's hard to find the right words when you're still untangling old stories and self-doubt. That's where your favorite AI assistant (hello, ChatGPT) can come in handy. Here's a simple prompt you can use to help generate *custom affirmations* based on your Confidence Audit and Five-Year Vision work:

## ChatGPT Prompt for Personalized Affirmations

Feel free to copy and paste this into ChatGPT directly!

"I'm working on rebuilding my self-confidence. Based on the

information below, please create ten personalized, empowering affirmations that feel realistic, motivating, and aligned with my goals.

Here's a quick snapshot of what I'm working on overcoming: [Insert top two to three fears, doubts, or confidence challenges from your Confidence Audit.]

Here's what I'm working toward: [Insert highlights from your Five-Year Vision: who you want to become, what you want to achieve, how you want to feel.]

Please craft affirmations that speak directly to these goals and challenges. Make them sound authentic—not cheesy or overly generic."

## Best Practices for Using Your Affirmations

- **Choose one to three at a time to focus on daily.**
- **Write them down by hand somewhere visible**—your journal, planner, a note on your mirror, and so on.
- **Say them out loud or listen to yourself saying them at least once a day.** Bonus points for saying them while looking at yourself in the mirror. I personally like to listen to recordings of myself listening to them through the free ThinkUp app while I put on my makeup and get ready for my day.
- **Anchor them to action by pairing them with your Confidence Reps.** (Example: If you're working on speaking up more, your affirmation could be: "My voice matters, and what I have to say adds value.")
- **Revisit and refresh your affirmations regularly—anytime your goals or fears evolve.** I personally like to revisit them quarterly, but I've had clients who prefer monthly, and some who prefer annually. Do what works best for you.

Confidence isn't built by wishing you felt differently. It's built by consistently telling yourself a new story—and taking actions that prove it true. One affirmation, one rep, one day at a time.

## Celebration Rituals

Many high-performing women achieve such incredible things but never give themselves the time or the space to actually celebrate themselves achieving them. They just move right on to the next thing. The problem with this is it never gives you the opportunity to anchor in the feelings of having done it, and through repetition anchor that feeling as your new norm.

Celebration rituals are purposeful acknowledgments of your progress, not just the individual outcomes. This could be as simple as journaling one win at the end of each day or pausing to honor a difficult conversation navigated with grace.

I'm going to share more about ways to journal your wins on a regular cadence in Chapter 8. Some examples of ways I've celebrated recent milestones include:

- **Getting a custom perfume formulated for hitting a revenue milestone.** Every time I wear it and smell it, I'm reminded of that feeling and motivated to do it again.
- **Taking a day off following completing a time-intensive project.** I do activities that fill my cup and give myself time to reflect on what a huge milestone I've accomplished.
- **Going out to dinner with my family to celebrate the signing of my book deal.** I had preplanned this prior to even the proposal for this book project to publishers. Throughout the entire proposal writing and submission decision process, I visualized how it would feel to do this with my family. It excited and motivated me! More on that in the next section.

- **Buying myself a piece of clothing that made me feel amazing to celebrate and wear to my largest speaking gig booked to date.** Now any time I wear it, I'm reminded of what a badass I am (never mind the fact I look amazing in it!).

When done right, celebration rituals emotionally anchor the feelings of a job well done, as well as motivate you to do it again. They also help your nervous system take time to adjust to the new normal of having achieved it, making it much less scary to go out there and do it again.

## Visualization Practices

Regularly imagining your future self—the woman who has already embodied the confidence you are cultivating—strengthens the neural pathways needed to turn vision into action.

One of my absolute favorite strategies to implement this is to create a vision board based on my Five-Year Vision. My very first ones were old-school—I'd save images from magazines or on Pinterest that resonated with me and represented each of the things I wanted to achieve in the next few years, and I'd cut them out and glue them onto a piece of foam core board. Since then, my process has evolved. Now, I build my vision boards digitally using Canva, and I include not just images but my favorite affirmations, quotes, and anything else that feels motivating and inspiring.

What you do next with this visual representation is most important. You want to make sure it's somewhere you see it each and every day. When I used physical boards, I kept them near where I got ready in the morning or by my desk where I worked. Now, I save digital versions as my laptop wallpaper and my cell phone lock screen, so I'm reminded of where I'm heading every single time I pick up a device.

While vision boards are a powerful visual anchor, real transformation happens inside your mind. I make visualization a part of my daily meditation practice. As I meditate each morning, I dedicate at least a third of my time to mentally rehearse my next level. I picture the version of myself who already has the confidence, the clarity, the energy I'm working toward. I see her walking into rooms, speaking onstage, writing, leading, living, and I ask myself: "What choices does she make today? How does she move? What does she believe?"

I also use the quiet time right before falling asleep for visualization. Scientifically, this is one of the best times to reprogram your subconscious mind. As we fall asleep, our brain waves naturally shift into a state called *theta*—a deeply relaxed, suggestible state—where our minds are more open to embedding new beliefs and ideas.[39] In other words, that short window of time between when your head hits the pillow and when you drift off is prime real estate for your dreams, both literal and metaphorical. Instead of letting my mind spiral through the stress of the day, I focus on replaying my goals and visions as if they're already real. I picture myself living them, feeling them, owning them.

High-performing athletes use visualization all the time for this exact reason. Olympians like Michael Phelps have famously used mental rehearsal to prepare for competitions—visualizing every stroke of the race, every turn, even setbacks like losing their goggles—before they ever touch the water.[40] Studies show that mental imagery activates many of the same neural pathways in the brain as physical practice does.[41]

This isn't wishful thinking. This is brain training. When you consistently visualize yourself embodying confidence, you aren't just imagining it—you're rehearsing it. You're building the mental muscle memory needed to step into it for real. And the best part? You don't have to wait to feel "ready" to start. You start by seeing future you first.

## Putting It All Together

### *Exercise*

# The Confidence Rebuild Framework

Confidence isn't something you either have or don't. It's a structure you build, piece by piece—especially when life, loss, or circumstance has knocked it down. The good news is you don't have to start from scratch. You simply need the right blueprint.

Here's a recap of the framework I teach my clients that includes all the tools I just shared with you, and the one I still return to myself when it feels like my confidence is waning:

## *Step 1:* Complete Your Confidence Audit

We can't rebuild what we're not willing to look at honestly. Identifying where you currently stand using the Confidence Audit you completed earlier was the first step. Now, take it one step further and ask yourself:

- What patterns do you notice across your answers?
- Are there environments, relationships, or situations where your confidence feels most diminished?
- Are there others where it feels naturally stronger?

Name these patterns. The goal isn't to judge them; it's to map them, so you can stop navigating your life blindfolded. Awareness creates choice; choice creates change.

## *Step 2:* **Craft Your Confidence Action Plan**

Once you know where the leaks are, it's time to start sealing them intentionally. Your Confidence Action Plan doesn't have to be complicated. In fact, it shouldn't be. The simpler, the better, because the goal is consistent action, not grand gestures.

Create a short list of one to three micro-actions you can take consistently to strengthen your sense of agency. Some examples might include:

- Speaking up once during a team meeting
- Sending a networking message to someone you admire
- Practicing saying "thank you" instead of deflecting a compliment

The key here is not volume. It's velocity. Small wins, stacked consistently, create momentum faster than sporadic bursts of effort.

## *Step 3:* **Implement Confidence Reps**

Think of confidence the same way you would think of training a muscle: It doesn't grow because you think about it; it grows because you use it.

Confidence Reps are daily, small actions designed to stretch you just outside your current comfort zone without overwhelming your nervous system. Feel free to adjust the reps to suit your needs. For instance:

- If speaking up terrifies you, your rep might be contributing once in a group chat.
- If self-promotion makes you squirm, your rep might be updating your LinkedIn profile to better reflect your achievements.

- If boundary-setting feels impossible, your rep might be saying "Let me get back to you" instead of defaulting to "yes."

It's not about being fearless. It's about building the capacity to take action even when fear is present. Consistency trumps intensity (more on this in Chapter 9). One rep a day is enough.

## Step 4: Sustain Your Growth with Anchor Tools

Building confidence isn't a one-time event. It's a long-term investment. That's why it's essential to create systems that protect the progress you're making—especially when life inevitably throws you a curveball.

Here are the anchors I recommend, but pick and choose whatever tools feel right for you:

- **Compliments File:** Keep a running document of positive feedback, wins, thank-you notes, and milestones. Review it any time your inner critic gets loud.

- **Personalized Affirmations:** Craft specific affirmations that speak to your real goals and values—not empty platitudes. (We'll workshop some in an upcoming section.)

- **Celebration Rituals:** Celebrate your micro-wins, even if it's just a mental note or a small treat. Reinforce the behavior you want to grow.

- **Visualization Practices:** Regularly imagine yourself embodying the version of you who has already achieved what you desire. Visualize not just the end result, but how she thinks, speaks, moves, and shows up today.

Think of these tools not as luxuries but as essential maintenance for the emotional architecture you are rebuilding.

Now remember, confidence doesn't grow in isolation. You can build the inner skills. You can do the personal reps. You can rewire your own belief systems. But if you're surrounded by the wrong people, even the strongest foundation can start to crack because confidence isn't just internal, it's relational. It doesn't matter how much confidence you have. If you choose to surround yourself with people who don't believe in you, who don't believe that what you want is possible, or who won't support you because it doesn't benefit them, you'll never, ever achieve your goals for yourself. Confidence needs the right soil to root and grow.

That's why the next culprit we're going to explore is Lack of Community or how your surroundings can either strengthen your courage or sabotage it when you need it most.

Let's dive in.

# Chapter Seven

# Lack of Community: You Are the CEO of Your Life—Curate Your Team Accordingly

*You are the average of the five people
you spend the most time with.*
—Jim Rohn

I couldn't believe what I was reading.

Around six months following my divorce, I had kicked and scraped enough money together to finally buy my own home, which was no small feat considering the divorce cleared me out of everything I had. Since I was the sole breadwinner, the majority of any savings we had (that I had made!) was awarded to my ex so he had something to "restart his life" with. So there I was, with sole custody of an infant, trying to figure out what the hell to do next.

I moved in with my family, over two hours away from my job, and had to grind out that horrendous commute five days a week that I mentioned in Chapter 5. All the while, instead of paying rent, I was banking every single penny (minus filling up my gas tank) I made toward the down payment to kick-start our new life. It was worth it, because in the end (and only six months later), I was sitting in the home of my dreams, in an amazing school district on Long Island.

While I should have felt amazing, truth of the matter was I felt pretty damn lonely. I was newly single after being in a relationship— albeit a bad one—for over fifteen years and now I was spending over twenty hours a week in my car by myself. I rarely ever got to have quality time with my son. I found myself with zero social connections and wasn't sure how to manage it.

Don't get me wrong, I still saw people daily. I spent time with people at work—the majority of whom were my family—and I loved that time spent with them. But none of them really understood, nor even thought to ask me, what I was going through at the time. It's easier to not address other people's personal challenges in workplaces so as not to make anyone else uncomfortable.

Then there was the topic of my friends, who are the ones you're supposed to be talking to about all the life transition stuff, right? All of my friends still lived in Brooklyn, three counties and a forty-five minute train ride away. If you've ever lived or spent any time in New York City, you know that the people who live in the five boroughs avoid leaving the city limits like the plague. Back when I was still living in Brooklyn, I had a friend in Manhattan who described their fifteen-minute subway ride to visit me just across the river as being like "trekking to Siberia."

And I felt a new sense of disconnection while visiting with the ones who actually made the ride out to see me and my new house on Long Island. It was as if I no longer had *anything* in common with them. It was not for the fact that I moved, but because I was a new mom and they weren't. I was the first of any of my friends to not only buy a house but to also have a kid. I spent a lot of time alone, but it wasn't for lack of trying. My son was still too young to attend school, so there was no opportunity to meet people there. I settled for the next best thing—I joined the local community Facebook group.

I had lurked there for months, reading comments and searching for reviews of places to check out. Anytime you could hear a helicopter in the area, everyone would flock to the group all at once, asking if they knew what the helicopter was doing and more times than not posting a meme or a GIF of Ray Liotta in *Goodfellas* outrunning the helicopters. It happened so often it got old after a while.

Earlier that day, I had been scrolling for restaurant recommendations when a woman who also happened to be a single mother had posted asking if anyone else in the group was a single mom. It immediately stopped my scroll.

*Holy shit! There's more of us,* I thought.

Reading through the comments, there were no less than a hundred responses. I was so excited, I didn't even think before dropping my own comment. It said: "I just moved here and I'm a single mom and have an eighteen-month-old. I didn't realize there were so many single moms in this community! Wouldn't it be awesome if we had our own group?"

I hit send, finished scrolling, and then got bored so I closed out the app for the day. That was until about fifteen minutes later when I heard the familiar *ping* that I had received a Facebook notification.

Upon opening it, I read the message and thought for sure that it was a joke. There was no way it could be real. *What the actual hell? I clicked faster than I ever had before. Was this real?* Yup. There it was: It was an alert sharing, "Congratulations! You are the new admin of the South Shore Single Mom's Group!"

Obviously, it had to be a mistake. I immediately clicked the link to read more about the group and saw that the original poster created it. I got a message from her directly maybe two minutes later.

"Hi, Corrie, and welcome to the neighborhood! I loved your idea, so I went ahead and created a group and added you as an admin. I'm excited to hear what ideas you have for it, so keep me posted!"

I froze, and panic and anxiety overtook me. I began to wonder, *Holy shit, I don't know these women! I haven't even lived here that long. Why would they pick me to do something like this? What if I meet them and I have nothing in common with them?*

This thought then made me pause and think—because it's ridiculous. "*Corrie*," I told myself, "you have *everything* in common with them. You're a single mom. This is a tremendous opportunity to finally meet people who know exactly what you are going through!"

It became clear as day for me in that moment what had been missing in my life during this time—the reason why I felt so alone and on an island (pun totally intended!) by myself!

My Overwhelm Culprit was Lack of Community. And I was not going to let this opportunity to meet other women just like me in my own community go to waste. Finding community didn't just happen by accident. It took a choice: to recognize what I needed, to take a risk, and to show up anyway.

In this chapter, I'm going to show you exactly how to do the same—no matter where you are or how alone you feel right now.

# When Your Circle Can't Carry You Forward or No Longer Exists

The famous motivational speaker Jim Rohn once said: "You are the average of the five people you spend the most time with." It's one of those truths that sounds simple on the surface, until you experience it for yourself.

When you're trying to create meaningful change, whether it's rebuilding after a loss, advancing your career, or stepping into a bigger vision for your life, the people around you can either fuel that growth . . . or they can quietly smother the fire out of it. But on the flip side? Losing your circle altogether can have just as devastating an impact.

Take research participant Aika, a pharmacist and newly single mother of three. During our conversation, she kept circling back to one painful theme: how isolated she felt. Not just from a time management perspective—having suddenly gone from a dual-parent household to doing it all alone—but also emotionally as she struggled to process her partner's infidelity and support her children while running on empty herself.

We bonded over a shared memory of what it's like to be too sick to parent—and have no one there to help pick up the pieces. One particularly painful and bittersweet memory of my own is when I came down with an awful case of the flu. At the time, I was lucky enough to have a live-in au pair, but luck doesn't always mean support. This particular au pair, the second of three I would host over those years, was selfish, narcissistic, and completely unconcerned with how her actions impacted anyone else. She was right there in the house. She saw I was ill. She could have stepped in to help care for my son or even just ask if we were okay, but she chose not to. That night, as I lay feverish and weak, it was my three-year-old son who tucked *me* into bed, kissed my forehead, and got himself ready for sleep. I remember feeling not just incredibly sick but profoundly guilty. It wasn't that I had no one around me—I had the wrong person—and I was still effectively alone.

That night taught me something I'll never forget: It's not just the presence of people that matters, it's the presence of the *right* people. Because here's the reality, especially if you currently have a circle: If the people around you don't support what you're working toward, don't believe it's possible, or don't know how to help you get there, continuing to prioritize them comes at a cost.

Most of us don't realize how isolated we've become until moments like these crack us open. We chalk it up to "just how things are," or blame the busy season of life we're in. We tell ourselves we should just be grateful for whatever support we have and silence the deeper ache for something more.

You can't outgrow your environment without outgrowing the version of yourself that expects you to stay in that environment. And you can't build a new future if you're clinging to an old circle that can't help you outgrow your environment.

In this section, we'll talk about why building an intentional, supportive community is essential, not just for your success, but for your ability to even envision success as possible.

## Growth Feels Lonely When Your Circle Isn't Growing with You

One of the biggest challenges women face when navigating change isn't just the external shifts; it's the sudden loneliness that creeps in when our old communities no longer fit the lives we're building.

Research participant Asami, a paralegal and mother of six, experienced this firsthand in multiple ways. Growing up, she witnessed her mother's struggles as a single parent, and those early experiences shaped both her relentless work ethic and the pressures she places on herself today.

At the time of our conversation, Asami was pregnant with her sixth child—a surprise pregnancy—and she worried deeply about how her growing family would be perceived at work: *Would her colleagues see her pregnancy as an inconvenience? Would her job stability be threatened?*

At home, the demands were just as heavy. Her husband's demanding career left her as the default parent for their children, one of whom had special needs. Add to that a strained relationship with her in-laws and minimal support from her own family, and Asami often felt like she was carrying the weight of the world alone.

The endless mental load, managing schedules, medical needs, emotions, and logistics left her exhausted. And even with therapy, she admitted how often she struggled with anger, frustration, and giving herself grace. She's not alone. According to the American Psychological Association's 2022 "Stress in America" survey, many adults reported needing more emotional support than they received in the past year, highlighting a widespread sense of isolation during challenging times. While it's not exclusively a gender issue, women are overwhelmingly expected to just suck it up and move on, often without the support systems they need, like paid maternity leave, affordable childcare, or flexible work policies to take the place of the village that used to exist to help raise a child.

When you're surrounded by people who see your growth as a threat, or simply don't understand it, it's easy to start questioning yourself. You wonder: *Am I asking for too much? Am I doing something wrong?* Then you begin to think, *Maybe this is just the way it has to be.*

But it isn't. And in the next section, we'll talk about why redefining your circle isn't selfish. It's survival.

## You Can't Borrow Belief from People Who Don't Believe It's Possible

No matter how strong your vision is, it's hard to keep reaching for more when the people around you can't, or won't, see it for you.

In my research interviews, one theme came up again and again: Women were hiding their ambitions to avoid judgment. I know exactly how that feels because I've lived it. Had I been surrounded by people who believed in my potential, I would have ended up on a very different career path.

As a young girl, I dreamed of becoming the (then) first female director to win an Oscar. I graduated college with a degree in production and even applied to the prestigious New York University film program for my master's. I was thrilled to learn I had been wait-listed—a huge accomplishment in itself—and was given the opportunity to be notified if a spot opened up.

When I shared this with my then-boyfriend (and later husband), he didn't celebrate. He questioned why I would even bother aiming so high. When the time came to decide whether to move forward, he talked me out of it. If I got in, it would mean moving to a new city, and he would either have to follow me or we'd have to break up. Rather than support my growth, he chose to clip my wings. And I let him.

It wasn't just personal. In professional environments, women face the same barriers.

According to the LeanIn.org 2023 Women in the Workplace Report, women are 24 percent less likely than men to report having strong sponsorship at work—meaning someone actively advocating for their advancement.

Without external encouragement, self-doubt festers. When no one around you is cheering, it's easy to start believing you have nothing to cheer for. And when you lose belief in yourself, it becomes even harder to find—or build—the community that could help reignite it.

## Logistics Struggles Make Building a New Community Feel Overwhelming

Even when we recognize that our current circle isn't serving us anymore, taking the leap to find new connections can feel overwhelming, especially for women already overloaded by the competing demands of work, parenting, and home life.

It's not that we don't want to get out there. We want to attend the conferences. We want to join the networking events. But logistically getting to the places where those opportunities happen isn't always feasible.

Take participant Amelia, a single mom and leadership professional in the staffing industry. During our conversation, she shared how clearly she sees the next level of her career, and how she knows her network is the key to unlocking it. She dreams of attending in-person conferences, building relationships, and finding the mentors who could help open doors. But the logistics make it nearly impossible. Overnight travel would require expensive, hard-to-find care for her young son. Most local networking events happen after hours, right when she needs to be at the soccer field, not at a cocktail hour.

When you don't have the village it takes to raise a child, and you're also carrying the full financial responsibility of keeping that roof over your heads, there's little room left for anything else.

Amelia knew that securing a promotion could drastically improve life for both herself and her son. But without the right connections, and without enough accessible opportunities, she felt stuck. When I asked her what she thought the solution could be, her answer was simple but powerful: more online resources that allow women to connect on their own time.

In fact, Amelia and I originally connected after she attended a virtual conference where I was a speaker. She was making every effort she could to expand her community, but she also admitted there simply aren't enough accessible options to create the momentum she needs.

Her story is echoed by countless others.

## Outgrowing Old Relationships Feels Like Betrayal—Even When It Isn't

Sometimes, the hardest part isn't building something new. It's letting go of what no longer fits.

We don't talk enough about the grief that comes with realizing people you once loved deeply no longer align with the person you're becoming. It can feel selfish, ungrateful, even cruel. But refusing to acknowledge that disconnect doesn't preserve those relationships; it just makes you smaller inside them.

Participant Chloe, an executive coaching client, shared that after stepping into a major leadership role, she found herself hiding her successes from longtime friends: "I didn't want them to think I was bragging. But at the same time, I felt like I couldn't talk about my life anymore without shrinking parts of myself."

Growth creates separation. That doesn't make you disloyal. It makes you honest. You're  not abandoning the people who were there for you; you're honoring who you're becoming. You don't have to settle for shrinking to fit spaces that no longer fit you. You don't have to stay stuck in isolation, waiting for the right people to magically appear. Building the community you need—and deserve—starts with one bold decision: Choose yourself first.

In the next section, I'll show you how to audit your current circle, expand your network in ways that feel authentic, and start surrounding yourself with the kind of support that does not hold you back but lifts you higher.

## *Exercise*

# Rebuilding Your Circle with Intention

When you realize your current community can't support where you're going, the solution isn't to blame yourself or even them. It's to choose, with care, who gets a front-row seat to your next chapter. You don't have to burn bridges. You don't have to make grand announcements. You simply have to start being as intentional about your relationships as you are about your goals.

In this section, I'll walk you through how to expand your community intentionally, nurture the relationships that nourish you, and gently let go—or lovingly loosen—the ones that don't.

## *Step 1:* **Conduct Your Community Audit**

Just like we did a Confidence Audit earlier, we need an honest look at who's in your circle right now—and how they're impacting your growth. Here's how to do it:

**Make a list of the five people you spend the most time with.** This could include friends, colleagues, family members, even social media connections you engage with often. If you are a parent or guardian of multiple children, your collective children count as one.

From there, you're going to make two columns next to their names. One headed "How are they helping me?" And one headed "How are they preventing me?"

In the "How are they helping" me column, for each person ask yourself:

- Does this person believe in the version of me I'm becoming?
- Do I feel energized spending time with them?
- Do they encourage my growth?
- Do they accept me for who I am, and can I be my full self around them?

In the "How are they preventing me" column, for each person ask yourself:

- Does this person prevent me from becoming who I'm meant to become?
- Do I feel drained spending time with them?
- Do they make me question my growth?
- Do they make me feel like I need to shrink, hide, or minimize who I am?

There's no judgment here. This is about observation, not blame. You're simply gathering information—because awareness creates choice.

## *Step 2:* **Understand That Letting Go Isn't Betrayal**

Some relationships are for a season, not a lifetime. That doesn't make them failures, it makes them part of your story.

After my move, I had friends I had known for decades who were hard to let go of, but letting go of them was necessary based on my new physical location as well as my new priorities in life (my son). If someone you once loved no longer fits the life you're building, you don't owe them guilt. You owe yourself honesty—and compassion for both of you.

Letting go doesn't always mean a dramatic goodbye. Often, it's about gently adjusting your time, energy, and expectations. When you're already stretched thin emotionally and mentally, even these small adjustments can feel daunting.

The reality is, setting boundaries with people you care about can bring up two of the Overwhelm Culprits at once: Lack of Confidence and Lack of Community—the confidence to believe you're allowed to prioritize your needs and handle difficult discussions and the community that believes you deserve to be surrounded by people who support you in doing so.

It's no surprise that one of the most common questions I get after my keynotes and workshops is: "How do I start setting boundaries without burning bridges?" You don't have to overexplain. You don't have to justify. You don't have to apologize for choosing yourself. But you can communicate your shift with kindness and clarity.

If you need language to lean on as you start having these conversations, here are a few simple examples:

**If you need to create distance without severing ties:** "Life's been really full lately, and I'm trying to be intentional about where I spend my time and energy. I care about you, and I hope you'll understand if I'm not as available right now."

**If you're outgrowing the relationship and want to transition it naturally:** "I'm working on some big goals that are pulling me in a different direction these days. I'll always be grateful for the time we shared, even if we're not in the same place anymore."

**If someone repeatedly pulls you into old patterns you're trying to leave behind:** "I'm making some changes in my life and focusing on a different path right now. I understand if we're in different places, and I'm wishing you well as I move forward."

**If someone questions or challenges you about being less available:** "I'm making some shifts to prioritize what's next for me. It's not personal, but it is necessary. I hope you'll respect that, even if it feels different than before."

You don't owe anyone a debate about your choices. You're not rejecting people—you're reclaiming your energy. And the people who are meant to continue walking beside you will understand that.

## QUICK CHECKLIST FOR SETTING BOUNDARIES WITH CARE

- **Clarity first:** Before you speak to anyone else, get honest with yourself by asking, *What boundary are you setting—and why does it matter?*
- **Keep it simple:** A few clear, heartfelt sentences are more powerful than overexplaining.
- **Lead with respect, not defense:** Assume goodwill unless proven otherwise. You can be firm and kind at the same time.
- **Hold the line:** If someone pushes back, you don't have to justify. Simply restate your boundary and move on.

Setting better boundaries isn't about being cold. It's about being clear and protecting the space you need to become who you're meant to be.

Now that you've created some capacity and space in your circle, in the next step, I'll show you how to start rebuilding it in a way that feels expansive, not overwhelming.

## *Step 3:* Expand Your Community in Ways That Feel Doable

Building a new circle doesn't require you to suddenly become a professional networker. (Spoiler alert: You don't have to attend a million awkward mixers either.)

You can expand your community in ways that feel doable, authentic, and aligned with the life you're living today, not the life you hope to have someday.

When I think back to the moment I was unexpectedly appointed admin of the South Shore Single Moms Facebook group, the growth didn't happen because I threw myself into every opportunity at once. It happened because I took small, consistent steps that fit the season of life I was in.

At first, all I did was post simple questions in the group and respond to the women who reached out in the DMs. Later, I started inviting moms to activities I was already doing with my son. Posts like: "My son and I are heading to the beach at one o'clock today—mile marker eight if you want to join!" That's it. No pressure. No formalities. Just an open door.

As the casual meetups grew, I started using the events feature to organize group outings: winery tours, apple-picking days, Mommy's Nights out. Eventually, the gatherings became so popular I had to start booking venues to accommodate the headcount. But none of it started with a grand plan. It started with one post, one invite, one connection.

When it comes to building your community, it doesn't matter how big the steps are—it matters that you're moving.

Here are a few ways you can start expanding your circle without overwhelming yourself:

- **Start small.** Attend one virtual event or join one online group aligned with your interests or goals.
- **Follow your curiosity.** If someone's work inspires you, reach out. A simple DM or email can spark a powerful connection.
- **Leverage what you already have.** Professional associations, alumni networks, book clubs, parenting groups—chances are, you're already connected to more potential allies than you realize.
- **Use asynchronous connection.** If real-time meetups are hard to swing, join forums, LinkedIn groups, mastermind programs, or online memberships where you can engage at your own pace.

You don't have to find a hundred people overnight. You just need to find your next one: one person who sees you, one person who believes in what you're building, one person who reminds you that you're not alone in this. Because when it comes to building a community that fuels your growth, consistency always matters more than speed.

## *Step 4:* **Create Your Community Action Plan**

Now that you've audited your current relationships and explored new possibilities, it's time to create a simple, doable action plan.

Ask yourself:

- What's one relationship I want to nurture more intentionally?
- What's one community or connection opportunity I want to explore?
- What's one boundary I want to set (even if silently) with a relationship that no longer serves me?

Pick no more than *three actions* to start. This isn't about doing everything at once; it's about choosing one or two threads to follow—and trusting they will lead to others.

## Closing Thought for This Section

Building a community that reflects your future, not just your past, is an act of leadership. It's also an act of self-love. You deserve to be surrounded by people who believe in your dreams as fiercely as you do, even on the days you doubt yourself. And the truth is, the more you choose yourself, the easier it becomes for the right people to find you.

## Putting It All Together

### *Exercise*

## You Are the CEO of Your Life. Curate Your Team

After moving into my new home as a newly single mom, I expected to feel proud, but instead I felt isolated. Having no friends nearby and no local support system, it was just me and my son, and a deep desire to find connection. All it took was my making a random comment on a passing Facebook post to connect to the exact kind of support I had been missing. That experience taught me that Community isn't *found*; it's *built* intentionally—one decision, one conversation, and one connection at a time.

Whether you're surrounded by people who don't believe in your vision, or you've lost your support system entirely, the result is the same: You're holding it all alone. And even if you technically *have* people around you, they may not be the *right* people. Aika's story, and mine, proved that the presence of people doesn't equal the presence of support. As women evolve, they often outgrow the communities that once felt like home.

Asami's story showed how changes in motherhood, career, and identity can leave you feeling like no one around you truly *gets* it. The truth? Most high-performing women aren't suffering from a lack of motivation—they're suffering from a lack of meaningful support. Ambition becomes dangerous territory when the people around you can't support it—or worse, actively discourage it. In my case, forfeiting my grad school opportunity because my partner couldn't support it changed the course of my life. In professional environments, this same lack of belief shows up through the absence of sponsorship and advocacy, which all too often leaves women to second-guess themselves in silence.

Even when you *want* to expand your circle, the real-life logistics often make it feel impossible. Amelia's story showed just how hard it can be to network when childcare, finances, and time aren't on your side. For many women, it's not confidence that's lacking, it's capacity.

One of the hardest parts of growth is realizing that the people who once "got you" no longer align with where you're headed. Chloe's story highlighted how success often brings separation, and how hiding parts of ourselves to keep others comfortable only makes the loneliness worse. Letting go doesn't mean cutting people off. It means making room for the support you need now.

So where do we go from here? The good news is you now have an easy-to-follow audit that will not only tell you more about the people you're choosing to surround yourself with right now but also give you the information you need to let go of the folks holding you back, to make space and capacity for meeting new people waiting to help boost you to your next level.

## Step 1: **Conduct your community audit.**

Get clear on who you're spending time with and whether those relationships are helping or hindering your growth.

## Step 2: **Understand that letting go isn't betrayal.**

Release what no longer fits—without guilt—so you can reclaim the space and energy to grow.

## Step 3: **Expand your community in ways that feel doable.**

You don't need to "network." You need real connection, one person at a time, in ways that work for you.

## Step 4: **Create your community action plan.**

Pick one person to nurture, one new connection to pursue, and one boundary to set. Keep it simple. Make it yours.

And the women I met through the South Shore Single Moms group? They didn't just listen. They didn't just understand. One day after seeing how exhausted I was, they secretly interviewed and hired a house cleaner to surprise me and lighten my load. That's the kind of support that changes everything. Whether personally or professionally, you are the CEO of your life, and these are the people you want on your team.

And the good news is, you get to choose them.

But here's the thing: No community—no matter how solid—can carry you if your own tank is empty. You are no good to others in your community if you're pouring from an empty cup.

That's why in the next chapter, we'll tackle the next Overwhelm Culprit: Lack of Conditioning—how to reclaim your energy, well-being, and capacity so you can actually enjoy the life you're building.

Let's take care of you. You're the one holding it all.

# Chapter Eight

# Lack of Conditioning: Even the Energizer Bunny Eventually Runs Out of Batteries

*When you don't put yourself first,
you're teaching everyone that you come second.*
—Mel Robbins

I had no idea how bad it had gotten—until staring at a lighthouse snapped me back to reality.

We all get the same 24 hours in a day and 168 hours in a week. But no matter how hard I tried, the math just wasn't mathing. Envisioning what a typical day should have looked like for me while working as an SVP revealed something like this:

**Eight hours sleeping (33 percent).** Let's be real, that was ideal but not happening. I was a solo mom with a baby/almost toddler.

**Four hours commuting (16 percent).** Yup! Two hours to get there and two hours back.

**Eight hours working (33 percent).** Again, this is ideal, but I was an executive, so it was usually more like 9 to 10 hours x 5 days a week.

**Two hours of chores (8 percent).** Someone's gotta make dinner, do the dishes, run a load of laundry, and pick up the house.

**One hour with my son (4 percent).** He had a crazy early bedtime, so I got some 1:1 time with him for maybe an hour daily.

**One hour for myself (4 percent).** If I was lucky, it usually was spent trying to have a semblance of a social life.

What ended up happening on the days I worked more than eight hours was that time had to come from somewhere else. More times than not, it came from chores or sleeping. Or on days where I didn't get eight hours of sleep due to my son having a sleep regression, it took me twice as long to function and get all the other tasks done because of, well . . . lack of sleep. So if I didn't sleep, I more than likely didn't pick up the house either and instead napped to make up for that lost time. It was an endless cycle of razor-thin time management margins and shuffling priorities daily. The problem was I'd become very efficient while running in this cycle. As a proud high performer, I kept going through this day in and day out and was completely blind to its impact on me, so much so that when my single mom friends pooled resources to get me a house cleaner, it confused me. I had honestly thought, *Everyone lives their lives like this: surviving and not thriving.*

I really had no reason to think anything was wrong at the time. I still had tremendous capacity and was turning out results that even surprised my therapist: new houses, promotions, landing big deals, dating again, rebuilding my social network. On paper I was killing it, so why should there be any reason to change anything?

I didn't finally see the situation for what it was until I was on a cruise with my family. Not the infamous one where I told everyone I quit my job and almost jumped off the balcony. This was a couple of years before that.

It was my first real vacation since my contentious divorce, and we were sailing from Canada down the Northeast coast back to our home base in New York City. My son was still small enough that I used to wear him in a baby carrier, and we spent seven full days exploring small coastal towns during the best weather of the year (I absolutely *adore* the fall and all the colors!) and spending the time with my family.

A thought hit me while overlooking the lighthouse in Portland, Maine, with my son close to me, him smiling and me still being able to smell his baby smell on top of his head as he snuggled against me. I can still see and hear the surroundings: the gorgeous flower beds circling the lighthouse still in bloom during the warm, early fall day; the crystal clear blue sky; the wispy clouds that floated effortlessly with the sea breeze; the soft crashing of the waves.

*"Holy shit! I'm actually present!"*

A couple of weeks earlier, I had been bawling by the side of my tub while giving my son a bath. I had been so excited that day to get to spend my hour a day with him and give him his bath, then get him to bed, so excited to break out his bath toys and have a splash fest with him. Instead, I found myself staring off into space, my mind wandering between traumatic memories I was still processing of the abuse I had just left and my to-do list I had to prematurely wrap up at work before the two-hour commute home. My son kept trying to get my attention, but in my zombie state, I was unresponsive.

When I finally snapped to it, I was so guilt and shame ridden. I so desperately wanted to be fully present with him and enjoy the moments I had. Every single day I'd make the intention to be fully present and every single day I was completely incapable of doing so.

At the lighthouse, I realized that's exactly where I was—present and absorbing all those tiny details I had been missing in small moments like this. It was like the lighthouse was the lightbulb my brain needed to realize what was actually going on.

It was obvious to me that I was enjoying that sightseeing moment because I love to travel. And in the process of being so busy being busy, I wasn't making any time for the things I love to do. And this was my own damn fault, because when you looked at how I'd spend a typical twenty-four hour day, I was spending a whole hell of a lot of time doing things for other people.

I was commuting four hours a day, working eight hours a day, doing chores for four hours a day, and caretaking for one hour a day. Every single time I was saying yes to someone else, whether that was accepting a pushed deadline or even a dinner invitation, I was saying no to myself. This is why I only had 4 percent of my entire day for me. It's also why my single mom friends thought to help take some of the two hours of chores off my plate, but I was still too busy to even see the difference it made, because I filled that time with other obligations for other people instead of myself!

I decided right then and there, when I returned home I was going to make a change. While sailing the seas, I even created a formal action plan and gave it a catchy name. I was preparing for the "Month of Me." I was going to go home, announce to the world I was dedicating thirty days to myself, *for myself,* and I was going to disconnect all social media and say no to any obligations that were not in direct alignment with my own personal well-being.

Little did I know at the time, my complete inability to be fully present was due to the fourth Overwhelm Culprit, Lack of Conditioning. I had gone far too long neglecting my own physical and mental health and wellness, and something had to change, because you can't lead, love, or live well if your mind and body are running on empty.

In this chapter, I'll help you identify where your wellness has been deprioritized—and give you the tools to begin reclaiming it, without shame, guilt, or needing to earn the right to rest.

## What Lack of Conditioning Is (and Why It Keeps You Stuck)

You can't pour from an empty cup. We hear it all the time. It's printed on tote bags and coffee mugs, offered as advice in therapy sessions and women's leadership workshops. But here's the truth most people don't say out loud: *Sometimes, we keep pouring anyway—because we don't think we have a choice.*

We don't mean to, but somewhere along the way, we've learned to prioritize everything and everyone else: the job, the kids, the chores, the obligations, the expectations. We've learned to measure our worth in output. We've became so damn good at over-functioning that exhaustion started to feel like a baseline. Being "tired but fine" became the answer we gave ourselves—and everyone else—until it wasn't.

Participant Amy (mentioned in Chapter 1) came into our conversation holding it together with white knuckles. On paper, she was thriving. She had recently been rated the top manager of thirty-seven people on the site, but behind the scenes her health was slowly declining. She used to be in great shape, running thirty miles a week, but now didn't have time for anything. As a result, she had gained weight and decreased her fitness.

When we talked about what her typical day looked like, it sounded eerily familiar: Wake up before dawn; get her son ready; rush to school drop-off; back-to-back meetings until school pickup; then dinner, bath, bedtime; then work again after her son was asleep. Maybe a late-night scroll on Instagram. Maybe a glass of wine. Definitely more work.

At one point, she said something that stuck with me: "A lot of the advice I've been given is decide where you're going to fail and then strategically fail. But what if you *don't* want to fail? I don't want to fail in my health. I want to work out. I want to eat right. I also don't want to fail in my home life either. I want to be there for my kids. I want to be there for my husband. And if I have to pick failing at work, I don't want to do that either, so I can't stop." She's not alone.

A 2023 study from Deloitte found that 53 percent of working women report higher stress levels year over year, with nearly half describing themselves as burned-out.[42] Yet most keep pushing forward, afraid that if they stop, even for a moment, it will all fall apart.

We get so used to being in motion that we forget how to be still. And the longer we stay disconnected from our bodies, our minds, and our deeper needs, the harder it becomes to hear ourselves at all.

The Lack of Conditioning Overwhelm Culprit isn't just about rest—it's about restoration. It's about asking: "How do I build a life that's actually livable? One where I'm not just surviving, but sustained?"

Because here's the hard truth: If your mind and body are depleted, no amount of strategy will save you. You can't make clear decisions when you're operating from exhaustion. You can't set boundaries when your nervous system is fried. You can't lead well—at work, at home, or in your community—when you haven't taken a moment to lead yourself.

## You Can't Change Your Life When Your Brain Is in Survival Mode

When you're overwhelmed, your brain doesn't ask, *What's next?* It asks, *Am I safe?* That's because chronic stress doesn't just wear you down, it rewires you. Literally.

When your nervous system is flooded with cortisol for too long, your brain shifts into survival mode. You become hyper-focused on short-term tasks and immediate threats because your body doesn't believe it's safe to plan for the future. It's too busy trying to protect you in the present. And when that becomes your default setting? It's nearly impossible to make aligned, strategic decisions. You're not stuck because you're incapable. You're stuck because your brain hasn't had the chance to fully exhale in months—maybe even years.

Participant Tara, a self-admitted, burned-out executive leader and mother of four, explained it this way: "My biggest frustration is trying to think how I want to think through this." She also reflected on the societal expectation that women should be able to handle stress seamlessly, without any acknowledgment that giving 100 percent at work leaves nothing left for home.

It wasn't ambition she lacked; it was capacity, because her brain had been in fight-or-flight for so long that anything beyond survival felt unreachable. She's not alone. The study "Cognitive Control and Flexibility in the Context of Stress and Depressive Symptoms," published in *Frontiers in Psychology,* found that individuals with lower cognitive flexibility under stress were more likely to experience psychological distress and difficulty adapting to challenges,[43] which is exactly what we need when we're trying to change our lives.

You can't access creativity when you're just trying to make it to bedtime. You can't build a new reality if your nervous system doesn't believe you're safe in this one. That's what Lack of Conditioning does. It keeps you so depleted mentally and emotionally that even the idea of change feels dangerous. Which is why the first step isn't to force your way forward. It's to restore your sense of safety, so your body and brain can finally believe that forward is even an option.

## You Can't Function If You're Physically Depleted

Your body is not a machine, but so many women treat it like one. We push through the exhaustion, we override the warning signs. We call headaches, tension, and digestive issues "normal." We caffeinate and white-knuckle our way through another day, telling ourselves we'll rest when things slow down while never fully admitting to ourselves that things never actually do.

Participant Lisette, the mother of two and a military organizational leader stationed in Alaska who was managing teams from the Atlantic to the Pacific coasts, broke down when I asked how she was feeling in her body.

She described the most painful part of her day as seeing the proof of her inactivity in the form of alerts on her fitness tracker, concrete evidence of how little time she had to care for herself. This created immense stress and anxiety, especially knowing she was heading into winter in Alaska, with twenty hours of darkness a day. She wasn't just worried about her physical health. She knew what this lack of movement would do to her mental state too. And she's not alone.

A 2022 meta-analysis published in *Preventive Medicine Reports* found that women who engage in regular physical activity experience significantly lower levels of depression and anxiety compared to those who are inactive.[44] The research also showed that even moderate levels of activity can improve mental health outcomes across all age groups, reinforcing just how essential physical movement is to emotional and psychological well-being—not just physical health. The irony is, the more depleted we are, the more likely we are to gaslight ourselves about it.

We tell ourselves:

- "It's just a busy season."
- "I'm lucky to be this needed."
- "Everyone feels like this, right?"

We've normalized depletion as a badge of honor. But the truth is, you cannot lead well, love well, or even live well if your body is running on fumes.

Lack of Conditioning doesn't just show up in extreme burnout or health crises, it's in the micro-decisions we make daily:

- Skipping meals because we're in back-to-back meetings
- Canceling workouts because someone else's needs feel more important
- Staying up late just to finally have a moment of quiet, even if it robs us of sleep

Over time, these small choices add up. And so does their impact: the sluggishness, irritability, inflammation, weight gain, and the slow erosion of vitality we once took for granted.

When we treat wellness like a luxury instead of a necessity, we pay the price with our health. And once our body breaks down, everything else does too—our relationships, our work, our energy— even our ability to dream beyond the chaos.

Reclaiming your health isn't selfish. It's the most strategic move you can make, because you can't sustain success in any area of life if your body can't keep up with your ambition.

## You Can't Think Clearly If You Don't Give Yourself Time to Think

In the absence of space, clarity can't survive. When every second of your day is filled with someone else's needs, deadlines, or notifications, it's no wonder you feel like you're sprinting through life on autopilot. Just as I was prior to my epiphany at the Portland lighthouse, you may be crossing things off your to-do list, but you're not really thinking—you're reacting.

Remember Laura, my executive coaching client from Chapter 3? She initially signed on to work with me after realizing she was in this exact scenario. She was a brand-new mom balancing sleepless nights with an infant and navigating a toxic workplace, who woke up one morning realizing she had absolutely no idea what she wanted the next phase of her career to look like. All she knew was she was unwilling to stay in the current phase she was in any longer than she had to, and she knew hiring someone to help facilitate those reflections would be helpful. That's the problem with constantly being "on." You lose access to the part of your mind that knows how to step back and see the bigger picture.

A 2015 study published in the *European Journal of Work and Organizational Psychology* found that participants who attended a one-day Cognitive Behavior Therapy (CBT) based workshop reported significantly lower levels of affective rumination and chronic fatigue six months later compared to those who did not attend the workshop.[45] This suggests that structured interventions can provide the mental space necessary for reflection and clarity.

Some of the most famous CEOs in the world understand this too. Bill Gates is known for taking an annual weeklong sabbatical at a cabin in the woods he refers to as his "Think Week."[46] He goes by himself, and that entire week he reads books and just, well . . . thinks. What began as quiet weeks spent at his grandmother's home evolved into a formal ritual that would later spark some of Microsoft's most innovative products. Internet Explorer was an idea that came out of his 1995 retreat.

There's something to be said about having a third space, one that's not home and one that's not work or the office, to be able to ruminate in a way that's different than your day-to-day life. Without time to process, your thoughts stay jumbled. Without time to reflect, your goals stay vague. And without time to breathe, your clarity disappears. This is why so many brilliant, capable women wind up feeling stuck—not because they lack ideas, but because they've created no space to hear them.

And even when we *do* get time alone, we often fill it with passive consumption:

- Mindless scrolling
- Podcasts in the background
- One more article about how to do life better

We're still taking in. We're not tuning in. Lack of Conditioning isn't just physical—it's cognitive. When your mind is constantly reacting, it never gets the chance to reconnect with what you *really* want, need, or know to be true.

If you want to make aligned, intentional decisions, you need a rhythm of reflection. That starts with reclaiming even just ten minutes a day to unplug from the noise and actually hear yourself think.

# You Can't Set Healthy Living Boundaries If You're Afraid to Say No

Let me be clear: Most women I work with *do* know what they need when it comes to their physical and mental health. The problem isn't awareness, it's access and oftentimes permission.

They'll say things like:

"I need to get back to the gym."

"I need ten minutes to myself without someone calling my name."

"I just need one weekend where I'm not 'on.'"

These aren't vague wishes. They're specific, repeated needs that have been buried under obligation, guilt, and chronic overextension. These women know what would help them feel better, but they've either lost the time, or they feel like they no longer have the right to claim it.

Of the research participants I've interviewed, over 17 percent explicitly mentioned being aware that their physical or mental health was suffering *but* they didn't have the time to do anything about it.

Some of the most common things these women said included:

"I know I need more sleep and to move my body, but there's no space in my day. I get up early for meetings, and once the kids are down, I just crash. It feels like I'm running on fumes."

—Executive Leader

"My therapist keeps reminding me to rest, but the truth is—I know I need it. I just don't know how to make it happen when I'm constantly needed by patients and my family."

—Healthcare Director

"I haven't been to the gym in months. I used to go three times a week, but work's been nonstop and I'm too drained by the time I get home. I can feel the difference mentally, but it feels selfish to take that time right now."

—Corporate Director

"I'm aware my anxiety is worse when I skip meals or don't go outside, but every time I try to schedule time for myself, something urgent pops up—for my team, my clients, or my kids."

—Entrepreneur

These participants aren't all lacking self-awareness. They're lacking the safety to act on what they already know. This is the trap of over-functioning as a high performer. We are so used to being the reliable one, the one who comes through, picks up the slack, and anticipates the needs of others, that it feels dangerous to step back—especially when your identity has been built around being the person who holds everything together.

But here's the hidden cost: Every time we say yes out of guilt or fear, we are unconsciously saying no to ourselves: to our rest, to our wellness, and to the very boundaries we know we need in order to thrive. This is where Lack of Confidence and Lack of Conditioning collide. Because if you don't believe it's safe to say no, if you're worried that doing less will make you seem weak, or flaky, or "not committed," then you'll never make space for the practices that restore you—even when you know what those practices are, even when your body is begging for them, even when your therapist, your coach, your partner, or your journal is telling you the same damn thing.

This isn't about selfishness. It's about sustainability. If you're serious about building a life that actually supports you, your boundaries can't just be suggestions. They have to be enforced. That means saying no without overexplaining. That means protecting your time like it's your most valuable asset, because it is. And that means recognizing that just because you *can* take something on doesn't mean you *should*.

If you don't make time to care for yourself, no one else will. And if you don't protect that time with clear, confident boundaries, it will be swallowed by someone else's priorities.

You already know what you need. I knew this too during my lightbulb moment staring at the lighthouse. The next step is making it nonnegotiable, which I'm going to help you do next.

## Creating a Life That Sustains You (Not Just One You Can Survive)

Here's the truth: Your health isn't a side hustle. It's the foundation that makes everything else in your life possible. If you want to lead well, love well, and live with clarity and purpose, you need practices that restore—not deplete—you. That starts with reclaiming your time and making your well-being nonnegotiable, but not in a performative, influencer-self-care way. We're not talking about a one-time spa day or a lavender-scented bath bomb you got on sale at Target. We're talking about a full-system reset, an intentional plan to remove what's draining you and reintroduce what sustains you—on your terms.

I call it the Month of Me. This is the exact thirty-day experiment I created for myself after that lighthouse moment. It's a structured, unapologetic commitment to myself and my health with no external obligations, no social media, no default yeses. It's just about space— just me—and committing time to the work of coming back home to myself. And now I want to help you create your own.

Before we dive into the strategy, though, we need to take stock of where you are—physically and mentally—so we can create a plan that's uniquely aligned with what *you* need.

## *Exercise*

# Conduct Your Physical Health Audit

Let's keep this simple—no tracking apps, no complicated plans—just an honest check-in between you and your body.

### *Step 1:* **Rate Your Physical Wellness**

On a scale of 1–10, how would you rate your current physical health and well-being, where 1 = Nonexistent and 10 = Thriving, no improvement needed? Don't overthink it. Go with your gut.

### *Step 2:* **Reflect on the Core Pillars**

Take a moment to consider how you feel in each of the following areas:

- **Hydration**—Are you drinking enough water daily?
- **Nutrition**—Are you fueling your body with food that supports your energy and mood?
- **Sleep**—Are you getting enough rest to wake up feeling restored?
- **Movement**—Are you moving your body regularly in a way that feels good?
- **Mental Health**—Are you feeling emotionally grounded, or are anxiety, stress, or depletion running the show?

## *Step 3:* **What's Working? What's Not?**

Make two quick lists:

- What's currently working well for your body?
- What's not working—and what's taking a toll?

Be honest. Be kind. This isn't about shame. It's about clarity.

## *Step 4:* **Choose One Thing**

Now, here's the most important part:

What's one thing—just one—you could start doing today that would improve how you feel physically?

Maybe it's drinking an extra glass of water. Maybe it's stretching before bed. Maybe it's eating lunch before 3:00 PM for once. The goal here isn't perfection; it's momentum.

Small changes add up—especially when you commit to protecting the time and space they require.

## *Exercise*

# Conduct Your Mental Health Audit

This isn't about a diagnosis. It's about awareness. Your mental and emotional state affects every area of your life—how you show up at work, how you connect with others, and how you care for yourself. But it's often the easiest to ignore because it doesn't always scream the loudest—until it does.

Let's take a moment to check in.

## *Step 1:* **Rate Your Mental Wellness**

On a scale of 1–10, how would you rate your current mental health and well-being, where 1 = Barely hanging on and 10 = Mentally strong, calm, and resilient? Don't sugarcoat it. Give yourself the truth without judgment.

## *Step 2:* **Reflect on the Pillars**

Consider how you've been feeling lately in the following areas:

- **Stress**—Are you managing stress in a healthy way or just pushing through?
- **Emotions**—Are you giving yourself space to feel and process or numbing and avoiding?
- **Rest**—Are you mentally resting or is your brain running 24/7?
- **Connection**—Are you supported or are you carrying everything on your own?
- **Self-talk**—Are your thoughts kind and helpful or critical and harsh?

## *Step 3:* **What's Working? What's Not?**

Jot down two quick lists:

- What's supporting your mental and emotional well-being right now?
- What's draining it—or what's missing entirely?

This part is about clarity, not perfection.

## *Step 4:* **Choose One Thing**

Ask yourself: "What's one thing—just one—I could start doing today to better support my mental health?"

Maybe it's taking five quiet minutes before you start your day. Maybe it's texting a friend. Maybe it's finally scheduling that therapy appointment. Maybe it's giving yourself permission to feel what you're feeling—without apology.

This one thing doesn't need to be big. It just needs to be yours.

*Exercise*

# Create Your Month of Me Plan

This isn't a vacation. It's a reclamation. Your Month of Me isn't about bubble baths and spa days—unless that's what you need. It's about consciously choosing to center your well-being for thirty days—to stop outsourcing your energy, to stop abandoning yourself in service of everyone else's needs—and choosing instead to start building a life that actually supports *you.*

When I decided to try this crazy experiment for myself immediately following my New England leaf-peeper cruise, I created a social media announcement sharing that for thirty days I'd be deleting my apps, and if anyone needed to get a hold of me, they could do so the semi old-school way—by calling or texting me. I deleted my social media, dating apps, and anything else I felt obligated to monitor and respond to, and then started drafting my plan.

For me, I felt a strong need to get re-attuned with my body and my mind. So I signed up for a thirty-day yoga challenge; committed to the Whole30 nutritional challenge; set up weekly appointments with my therapist; and signed up for a weekly meditation class at my local Buddhist center.

Now, let's map it out for you.

## *Step 1:* **Set Your Intention**

Before you dive into logistics, get clear on *why* you're doing this. Ask yourself:

- "What do I want this month to feel like?"
- "What part of me needs the most care right now?"
- "What's the consequence if I keep going the way I've been?"

Write down your core intention in a sentence or two. This is your anchor.

## Step 2: Choose Your Focus Areas

Using your audit findings, pick three to five focus areas that support your mental and physical well-being. These will guide your commitments.

Some examples:

- **Nutrition**—Whole foods, hydration, fewer processed meals
- **Movement**—Daily stretching, walking, or a short fitness challenge
- **Mental health**—Therapy, journaling, quiet time, or meditation
- **Social detox**—Taking social media off your phone or setting app limits
- **Sleep**—Establishing a consistent bedtime and wind-down routine
- **Creative space**—Reading, writing, or creating without a purpose

Not every activity you do needs to have a goal or revenue tied to it. This isn't about overhauling your life and routine—it's about choosing what matters most for this season only. Remember, this is a thirty-day experiment, not a commitment for life.

## Step 3: Set Your Boundaries

Decide what you're *not* doing this month. This might include:

- Saying no to invitations that feel draining
- Canceling or pausing unnecessary obligations
- Avoiding people, platforms, or projects that pull you away from your focus areas

This is your permission slip to *not* be available for everything and everyone.

I know for me, I decided I was going to say no to any social invitations that would have me out past 10:00 PM. That way, I could remain confident I'd hit my sleep goals and still have enough energy to complete my thirty-day yoga challenge in the morning.

## *Step 4:* **Choose Your Substitutions**

Now ask: "What could I *replace* those things with?"
Some examples:

- Replace thirty minutes of scrolling with thirty minutes of reading.
- Replace a rushed breakfast with a leisurely, mindful one.
- Replace a nightly binge-watch with a walk, bath, or early bedtime.

Small swaps add up. You're not trying to do more. You're trying to do *different*.

## *Step 5:* **Make It Public (If That Helps You)**

When I did my first Month of Me, I announced it publicly, because that kind of declaration helped me stick with it. You don't have to tell the world. But sharing it with a few key people (or even just writing it down where you'll see it daily) can give you the external accountability you need to follow through.

## *Step 6:* **Protect It**

Put your Month of Me in your calendar. Treat it like a nonnegotiable project, because it is. It's a commitment to yourself and it's your responsibility to hold yourself accountable to it. And if life throws something at you? That doesn't mean you failed. Adjust with intention. Come back to your anchor. Keep going. This isn't a detox. It's the first step in designing a life that doesn't require you to escape from it.

Exercise

# Communicating and Protecting Your Boundaries

If you're serious about reclaiming your time and your health, you can't just *set* boundaries. You have to *communicate* and *protect* them.

This is where so many women struggle—not because they don't know what they need but because they're afraid of what will happen if they prioritize it out loud. They're afraid they'll disappoint someone; let someone down; be seen as selfish, inflexible, or worse—replaceable.

But if you want your Month of Me to actually work (or any future version of it), you have to stop internalizing other people's discomfort as your responsibility. Boundaries aren't walls. They're instructions. They teach people how to treat you.

Here's how to make yours clear—and enforceable.

## *Step 1:* Decide What Needs to Be Communicated (and to Whom)

Not everyone needs to know your full Month of Me plan, but anyone who will be impacted by your new commitments—a partner, your team, your kids, or your best friend—deserves a heads-up.

Ask yourself:

- "Who might be confused or hurt if I don't explain this shift?"

- "Who might unintentionally cross a boundary if I don't define it clearly?"
- "Who can actually help hold space for my goals if they understand them?"

Proactive communication prevents reactive resentment.

## *Step 2:* **Choose the Right Script**

You don't owe anyone a PowerPoint presentation on why you're making changes. You just need a few honest, clear sentences that explain what you're doing and what you need from them.

Here are some scripts you can use or adapt:

- **To a partner:** "For the next thirty days, I'm focusing on rebuilding my energy and well-being. That means I'll be carving out time for myself in the evenings. I'd love your support in helping me hold that space."
- **To a friend or colleague:** "I've committed to a short reset this month to focus on my health. I may be a little less available than usual, but it's only temporary and really necessary."
- **To your kids or family:** "Mom is taking better care of herself this month so she can be an even better mom. That means I'll be doing some new things in the mornings/evenings. It's not forever, and I'd love for you to cheer me on."

The goal here isn't to ask for permission. It's to lead with clarity and kindness.

## *Step 3:* **Anticipate the Pushback**

Some people will be confused—some might be annoyed—especially if they've gotten used to the overextended version of you who never said no. That's okay. You are not responsible for managing anyone else's feelings about your boundaries. What you *are* responsible for is staying in integrity with your needs—even when someone else doesn't understand them yet.

If someone pushes back, you can calmly say:

- "I get that this is different than what you're used to. But it's important to me, and I need you to respect it."
- "This isn't a rejection of you—it's a commitment to myself."
- "I'm not available for that right now. I hope you'll support me anyway."

If they don't, that says more about them than it ever did about you.

## *Step 4:* **Prepare to Hold the Line (Even When You Want to Fold)**

You will be tempted to break your own boundaries, especially when the guilt creeps in, especially when someone needs something "just this once." That's normal. But here's what I want you to remember: *Every no to them is a yes to yourself.*

And that yes? That's how you get your time back, that's how you reclaim your health, that's how you begin to live a life that doesn't break you down before it builds you up. Boundaries turn your Month of Me from a cute idea into a transformational practice.

You already know what to do. Now it's time to protect your right to do it.

## Putting It All Together

### *Exercise*

# You Can't Lead Well
# If You're Running on Empty

I didn't realize how far I'd fallen out of alignment with myself until I was staring at a lighthouse with tears in my eyes. That moment of presence, surrounded by sea air and fall blooms, snapped something into focus: I had been outsourcing every hour of my life to everyone else's needs, and calling it ambition.

The truth is that many high-performing women don't reach burnout because they're weak. They reach it because they're strong, and because they've been taught to stay in motion even when their bodies and minds are begging for a pause. This is the hidden cost of Lack of Conditioning: You're exhausted, depleted, and overwhelmed, not because you don't care, but because you've been conditioned to believe your needs don't matter.

You saw this in Amy's story, where the pressure to succeed at home, at work, and in her health left no safe place to fall short. You saw it in Tara's story, where the stress was so relentless her brain couldn't even think clearly. You saw it in Lisette's story, where the absence of movement in her day was quietly breaking down both her physical and emotional well-being. And you saw it in Laura's story, where the noise of life drowned out her own desires, until she finally carved out space to hear them.

Here's what we know now: You can't change your life when your brain is in survival mode. Chronic stress keeps your nervous system in a constant state of threat, which makes strategic thinking and creativity feel impossible. You're not stuck because you're failing, you're stuck because your brain doesn't feel safe enough to imagine something different. You can't function if you're physically depleted. When your body is overworked and under cared for, even simple choices feel like mountains to climb. Skipping meals, losing sleep, and deprioritizing movement all add up and slowly begin to erode your energy and vitality.

You can't think clearly if you don't give yourself time to think. When you're always reacting, you lose access to reflection. Even ten quiet minutes a day can start to shift your mental clarity in powerful ways. You don't need more input. You need more space.

You can't set healthy boundaries if you're afraid to say no. Most women I work with already know what they need. What they lack is the safety—and the permission—to protect it. Every *yes* to someone else is a potential *no* to yourself, and when you make that trade enough times, it catches up with you.

That's why I created the Month of Me, a thirty-day experiment in self-reclamation—not (another) vacation, not a spa retreat—a deliberate and strategic reset to reconnect with your body, your mind, and your own damn needs, to stop abandoning yourself, and to start choosing yourself again.

Now, you've got the tools to build one for yourself.

## *Step 1:* Conduct Your Physical Health Audit

Check in with your hydration, nutrition, sleep, movement, and energy. Identify what's working, what's not, and one small change you can make today.

## *Step 2:* Conduct Your Mental Health Audit

Rate your stress, rest, emotions, connection, and self-talk. What's supporting your mental health—and what's silently draining it?

## *Step 3:* **Create Your Month of Me Plan**

Design a thirty-day experiment based on your needs. Set your intentions, choose your focus areas, create your substitutions, and protect your time.

## *Step 4:* **Communicate and Protect Your Boundaries**

Decide who needs to know. Use clear, honest language. Anticipate pushback, and hold the line with self-trust and compassion because boundaries aren't selfish, they're strategy. The most successful, fulfilled women I know don't just work hard. They take care of themselves like it's their job—because it is.

Now that you've learned how to stop abandoning yourself in the name of over-functioning, we're going to tackle the next and final Overwhelm Culprit, Lack of Consistency.

Even when you set out to improve your fitness and are working toward six-pack abs, you can't just work out once and expect them to appear. The best intentions won't stick unless you build the habits and systems that help you show up sustainably.

Let's turn your momentum into a lifestyle. You're ready!

# Chapter Nine

# Lack of Consistency: Extraordinary Lives Require Extraordinary Action

*We are what we repeatedly do.*
*Excellence, then, is not an act, but a habit.*
—Aristotle

I could not believe she'd even ask me that.

It had been six months following my divorce. I was sitting in the office of my therapist, Elizabeth, at my weekly appointment when she suddenly dropped what felt like the most absurd question of all time: "Corrie, have you considered dating again?"

The question stunned me into silence. When I finally processed the audacity of it, I let out a laugh.

"No," I said. "It's been the last thing to even cross my mind."

I mean, *come on*. I had just been entirely cleared out financially. I was commuting twenty hours weekly while trying to save up for a new place to live. I was hanging on by a threadbare thread. She knew all of this; it's not like we hadn't talked about the toll that stress had taken on me.

She didn't say anything, just sat with me in the silence.

After a couple contemplative moments, I finally asked, "What makes you think I'm even ready for something like that?"

"Believe it or not, you're ready," she said. "You've been grieving the loss of that relationship for years—even before the divorce. Over the past six months, you've done the work. You've dug into what brought you into that relationship to begin with. And you've mentioned more than once that you don't want your son to grow up an only child. You've said you want a partner who will love and care for you and your son the same way you give love and care to others. You're in a really strong place to start looking for that, if that's what you want."

*Wow*. I had never thought about it that way. I took a beat to let it all sink in.

"As amazing as that sounds," I finally said, "I have no idea where to even start."

"What's holding you back?" she asked.

"Honestly? Time," I told her. "I know how I ended up in my last relationship. I was in college and working at a restaurant. I wasn't looking for love. He just kept showing up and eventually I gave in. There was no intentionality to it. I didn't even know what I wanted in a partner back then. I was young, naïve, and operating on autopilot. Now, I know I need to be far more selective. But that also means putting in way more effort—and I have no idea where to fit that in."

Elizabeth didn't skip a beat. "We make time for the things that are a priority to us," she said, "and if finding love is a priority, then I know you'll figure it out. You always do."

She wrapped up our session, and I left her office still thinking about what she'd said. I climbed into my car and started the two-hour drive back to Long Island. My usual podcast started playing through the car speakers, but I shut it off. My mind was already buzzing.

*Could I really do this?* I ran through the logistics in my head. I had at max one night a week when the au pair worked late. That was it. That was my window. It didn't feel like much, but it was something.

The problem wasn't that I didn't want to date. The problem was that I didn't have a system to support it.

That's when my SVP brain kicked in. I started thinking about a marketing project we were working on at the time—testing messaging for a new product line. We were optimizing copy and targeting at every level of the funnel: awareness, prequalification, and conversion. We weren't just throwing things at the wall. We were tracking every move, every result, and refining our plans based on the data.

*I could do that with dating.* I didn't need bars or setups. I had the Internet. I could treat dating like a campaign. Build a strategy. Test the variables. Refine the process. Optimize for the right kind of person. I didn't have to guess. I could systematize.

My plan was simple: Try multiple online dating platforms. Create a profile that was so uniquely and unapologetically me that it would act as a magnet—and a filter. I'd attract the right people and repel the wrong ones. I'd spend fifteen minutes a day reviewing matches, responding to conversations, and prequalifying prospects. If the connection seemed promising, I'd schedule a quick meetup—coffee or a cocktail. If it clicked, great. If not, I'd return to the queue.

It was dating, yes. But it was also a habit, a system, a ritual of showing up for the version of my future I wanted most.

I didn't realize it at the time, but what had overwhelmed me wasn't the idea of dating. It was the inconsistency. I knew what I wanted. I knew the kind of person I was looking for. I even knew the traits I was determined to avoid. But I didn't believe I had the capacity to take consistent action. I thought I had to go all-in or not at all.

That was the real culprit: Lack of Consistency, because if you don't believe small steps will get you anywhere, you won't take them. And when the only options you give yourself are perfection or nothing? Nothing always wins.

That's what this chapter is here to solve. In the pages ahead, I'm going to help you:

- Uncover the hidden ways inconsistency is sabotaging your energy, productivity, and confidence,
- Identify the mental blocks that keep you from following through,
- Build personalized, sustainable systems that actually work with your life, and
- Stop the all-or-nothing cycle and create repeatable habits that stack over time.

Because consistency isn't just about discipline. It's about making it easy to do what you said you'd do, even if you're tired, even if life gets messy, even if your entire day goes off the rails.

The women I coach aren't failing because they're lazy or unmotivated. They're failing because they're exhausted, and they don't have a system that holds them when their capacity drops. That changes now.

Let's build something together that doesn't just work on your best day but also on your worst. Let's make success feel sustainable. Let's finally close the gap between what you say you want and what you actually do.

## Why You Feel Stuck (Even When You're Trying)

You're not lazy, you're not flaky, and you're definitely not lacking motivation. But when your goals feel forever out of reach—despite how badly you want them—it's easy to start wondering if something is just . . . *wrong* with you.

You make the vision board.

You buy the planner.

You listen to the podcast.

You tell yourself, *"This time it's going to be different."* And for a few days—or maybe even a few weeks—it is.

Then something happens. Life gets chaotic. Someone needs you. A deadline pops up. A kid gets sick. You miss a day. Then another. And just like that, all that motivation you started with evaporates. This is when most women start blaming themselves.

But here's the truth: The issue isn't your discipline; it's your *system*.

We're taught that change is about willpower—just try harder, just do it, just push through. But real consistency, the kind that builds momentum and lasting results, doesn't come from trying harder. It comes from building the right container.

And when that container doesn't exist? Of course you fall off track. Of course you struggle to sustain progress, especially if no one's holding you accountable except yourself.

Let's be honest—self-accountability is one of the hardest things in the world to master. Not because you lack integrity, but because your life is already packed with priorities that shout louder than your own voice.

Without a clear system, it's easy to:

- Start strong but stall out when the novelty wears off.
- Spiral into guilt after missing one or two days.
- Struggle to pick the habit back up once you've "broken the streak."
- Abandon goals entirely because they feel like more work, not less.

And when you live in a world that constantly demands your time and attention, it's nearly impossible to stay consistent if you don't have built-in ways to simplify, automate, and track your progress.

That's the problem this chapter will help you solve. Because you don't need another big, sweeping plan to overhaul your entire life, you need a simple, repeatable structure that can hold your habits—even when life gets chaotic—a rhythm you can return to, over and over again, until consistency becomes second nature.

We're going to build that together—starting with small, sustainable changes that actually fit into your real life. Because consistency doesn't require perfection. It just requires a process that supports you.

## You're Not Unmotivated—You're Unstructured

If you've ever told yourself, *"I just need to try harder,"* I want you to stop right there. Because the problem isn't your effort, it's your system. The truth is, success is built upon the consistency of small, incredibly boring actions done over time.

When we don't have clear structures in place to support our goals, it doesn't matter how motivated we are, we will eventually burn out.

And then we'll start the cycle all over again: Set the goal, make a plan, fall off track, feel guilty, repeat. It's not that you're lazy. It's that no one ever taught you how to build a system that works for your life as it is. You've been trying to build momentum on a shaky foundation and blaming yourself when it cracks.

I see this all the time with my coaching clients. They have incredible vision. They know what they want. They might even know *why* they want it. But when it comes to showing up for themselves every day in pursuit of that goal? They're winging it. They're reacting to their calendars, their kids, their coworkers—hoping that eventually things will calm down long enough for them to focus. They're building castles on quicksand.

Participant Takara, a mother of two, shared with me about the pain she had experienced being overlooked for promotions despite training others who were promoted over her. She described having a panic attack triggered by the stress of managing work and caregiving simultaneously. After struggling with feelings of guilt and an identity crisis, she questioned her value and role and ultimately decided to step away from her job to focus on her family. As someone who thrives on structure, she found it difficult to manage the unpredictable demands of both work and parenting, especially when sidelined by employers who did nothing to accommodate her needs. Sound familiar?

It's not that Takara didn't care about her goals. In fact, she was devastated and ashamed for stepping away from the work she loved. It's that she had no system to support them—no process to hold her steady on the days she was tired, overwhelmed, or unsure where to start. And those are the days that matter most, because consistency doesn't thrive in ideal circumstances. It thrives when the process is so embedded into your life that it happens even when conditions aren't ideal.

But it's not just the schedule that breaks us. It's the constant mental friction of decision-making, without support, space, or structure. Without structure, your brain will always default to what's easy, familiar, or urgent—not what's important. And when that happens enough times, your system doesn't just break, your confidence does too. This is what psychologists call "decision fatigue," and it's a major reason smart, motivated women fall into stop–start patterns, even when their goals matter deeply to them.

## You Don't Need More Willpower— You Need Fewer Decisions

If you've ever found yourself mentally exhausted before the day even begins, you're not alone. The concept of decision fatigue explains this phenomenon: Our brains have a finite capacity for decision-making each day, and once depleted, our ability to make quality choices diminishes.

For women, especially those juggling caregiving responsibilities, the mental load is disproportionately heavy. A 2023 study by the National Centre for Social Research shows that women handle 71 percent of household tasks that require mental effort and often bear the brunt of household and caregiving decisions, leading to chronic stress and burnout. This is compared to 45 percent of fathers taking on household decisions.

So, how can we combat this? By reducing the number of daily decisions we need to make, we can conserve mental energy for what truly matters. Implementing systems and routines can be a game changer.

Consider the approach of successful individuals like Steve Jobs, who famously wore the same black turtleneck and jeans daily to minimize decision-making. While this strategy is well-documented among male entrepreneurs, female leaders are also adopting similar practices.

Designer Misha Nonoo introduced the Easy 8 collection, a capsule wardrobe designed to simplify dressing decisions for busy women. The concept uses a limited number of essential, interchangeable clothing items. By curating a selection of versatile pieces, women can reduce the time and energy spent on outfit choices, freeing up mental space for other priorities. Understandably, this has gained popularity among women seeking to streamline their lives.

Beyond clothing, automating meal planning, setting consistent routines, and delegating tasks where possible are all strategies that can reduce decision fatigue. Essentially, it's not about mustering more willpower; it's about creating an environment where fewer decisions are necessary. By establishing systems that minimize daily choices, we can alleviate the mental load and focus our energy on achieving our goals.

## You Keep Overcommitting to Things You Can't Sustain

Here's the hard truth about most of the women I work with: Their problem isn't laziness. It's overcommitment. They say yes to *everything*—big opportunities, small favors, last-minute requests, volunteer roles, late-night Slack pings, one-more-thing-on-the-calendar—not because they have the time or energy . . . but because they believe they *should*—and then they wonder why nothing gets done the way they intended.

Overcommitting is sneaky like that. It *feels* productive. It *looks* like enthusiasm. But really, it's a trap, a pattern that gives the illusion of progress while robbing you of the consistency you actually need to reach your goals. What's even worse? You're not even in control of your own overcommitment and the consistency you actually need to reach your goals. Just ask Rebecca.

Rebecca had recently had a baby, yet her boss expected her to be in the office seventy hours a week. No matter how hard she tried, she struggled to make it work and that was having a devastating impact on her mental health. She felt frustrated with the lack of support and opportunities she'd lose by not making herself available all that time. Meanwhile, her own goals, like landing a promotion and improving her physical health, kept slipping to the bottom of the list.

"I swear I'm trying," she told me. "I've struggled to make myself available when they need me so I can still be visible enough for these opportunities and somehow squeeze in a walk. But every week something else takes over—a client crisis, a sick kid, a committee call that runs long—and then I just give up." She ended our conversation by sharing she was actively searching for a new remote role that wouldn't demand so much of her capacity.

Rebecca was struggling, not because she didn't care, but because she was expected to juggle more than anyone should be expected to carry. Sound familiar?

The truth is, consistency requires capacity. If you (or someone else like Rebecca's boss) are filling every inch of your schedule with obligations and then wondering why there's no room for your own goals, it's not a time management issue—it's a boundary issue.

We overcommit for all kinds of reasons:

- Because we don't want to let people down
- Because we feel guilty prioritizing ourselves
- Because we believe that if we *can* do it, we *should*

- Because we think saying yes will make us more liked, respected, or valued

But every *yes* you give without intention becomes a *no* to something else—often to your rest, your recovery, or your real priorities. And here's the kicker: The things we overcommit to are usually the first things to suffer when we're overwhelmed. You start skipping workouts. You stop doing your morning journaling. You put your dream project on pause because someone else needs you again. The inconsistency isn't a discipline problem. It's a capacity problem.

Until you get honest about what you *can actually sustain*, your progress will keep getting sidelined. That's why building consistency isn't about doing more. It's about doing less—with more intention. You can't make real change if you're burning out in the process.

So, before you add another thing to your calendar or reflexively say yes, ask yourself: *Can I actually sustain this?* And if the answer is no, don't force it. That doesn't make you flaky—it makes you smart because the most powerful commitments you can make . . . are the ones you keep.

## You Don't Have a Way to Track Progress That Works for You

Here's the trap most high-achieving women fall into: They set ambitious goals, hit the ground running . . . and then slowly lose momentum, not because they're incapable, but because they have no idea whether they're actually making progress. This isn't about laziness. It's about feedback or, rather, the *lack* of it.

When you're juggling a demanding career, a family, and everyone else's needs, your brain is scanning constantly for signs of success. And when it doesn't see clear evidence that what you're doing is *working*, it gets discouraged fast. That's why so many women start out strong and then burn out midway. They're doing the work, but because they don't have a simple way to track their progress, it feels like nothing is happening, so they quit. It's not that *they* failed. It's that their system failed *them*.

Participant Denise is an ambitious mom of two and a small business owner. As a team of one, she handles all her own targets and goals, which she found overwhelming because she's doing it for both her family and her business. She's juggling her career, childcare, house cleaning, managing the family calendar, and more, which is leading to mental exhaustion.

"I have this big vision, and I keep telling myself I'll do one thing each day to move it forward," she said. "But I never have the time to plan. No timeline. No idea whether I'm actually getting closer or just spinning my wheels. Eventually, I lose steam—not because I don't care, but because I don't see anything changing and my time is better spent elsewhere." She's not alone. Most of us were never taught how to track our own growth—especially in areas that don't have obvious metrics like weight loss, finances, or grades. We rely on the big milestones to validate our effort. And when those don't come fast enough, we tell ourselves we're not doing enough, even if we're actually doing *a lot*.

But here's the thing: The more invisible your progress feels, the harder it is to sustain. That's why we need systems that reflect the *truth* of our effort—not just the outcomes. You need a way to measure movement that works *for your brain, for your life*, and *for your goals*, not some aesthetic planner that makes you feel behind every time you open it, not another complicated tracking app that stresses you out more than it helps, not someone else's productivity system that doesn't fit your capacity or season.

You need a tool that shows you where you're winning—even when the wins feel small, because progress isn't always loud. Sometimes it looks like showing up on a day you wanted to give up. Sometimes it looks like rest. Sometimes it's just the fact that you *kept going.*

Later in this chapter, I'll introduce you to the exact framework I use to track my own goals and the system I give my clients to do the same. But for now, here's what I want you to remember: If your progress isn't being tracked in a way you can see, feel, and believe in, it's going to *feel* like you're failing, even when you're not. And that's a consistency killer every single time.

## You're Doing It Alone (and Accountability Is Everything)

Here's something most high-performing women won't admit out loud: They're tired of holding it all together alone. It's not that they don't know what to do. It's that they're doing it without backup, without anyone asking how it's going, without anyone reminding them to stay the course, and without anyone saying, "Keep going. You're doing great."

Of the women I've interviewed in my research project, nearly half of them—47 percent—explicitly said that the one thing they were missing was accountability, support, or a community of like-minded women.

Their own words said it best:

- "I need a community of working women who get it. I want to feel like I'm not the only one doing this alone."
- "I just want someone to check in with me to make sure I'm actually making progress."

- "I want a program that includes real support—not just content. I need help following through."
- "Honestly? I need someone to call me out when I start slipping back into old habits."

What's so interesting is they knew they needed accountability; what they didn't realize is that they could also create it for themselves.

Because here's the secret: External accountability can jump-start your momentum, but *internal accountability is what sustains it.* That's why so many women stay stuck in stop–start cycles. They make progress when there's a deadline, when someone's watching, when a boss is checking in, when a partner's depending on them. But when the structure disappears, so does the follow-through.

It's not a discipline problem. It's a dependence problem. You've been conditioned to only show up when someone else is counting on you. But what if you learned how to count on yourself? What if your progress didn't hinge on whether someone texted to remind you, or a group thread was active, or a coach followed up? What if the structure, the rhythm, the accountability didn't have to come from a coach, a calendar, or a crisis? What if it could live inside you—and actually *stay* there?

You weren't born knowing how to build that kind of consistency. None of us were. But you *can* learn. And that's exactly what we're going to do next.

## You're Waiting to "Feel Like It"

We all do it. You tell yourself you'll start when you're less tired, when you're more motivated, when work slows down, or when life feels a little easier. You wait for the energy to strike, for the spark to return, for that elusive sense of readiness to finally arrive. But here's the problem: Consistency has *nothing* to do with how you feel. If you're waiting to "feel like it" before taking action, you might be waiting forever because motivation is unreliable, energy is unpredictable, and inspiration is fleeting. And the more chaotic your life is—the more responsibilities you juggle—the less likely it is that the stars will ever align perfectly. That's why so many brilliant women get stuck. It's not because they don't know what to do, but because they're trying to run their lives on emotion instead of structure.

Participant Alexis put it this way: "I know I want to write a book, but I'm always waiting for the time when I feel focused and inspired. The problem is that time never comes. I keep telling myself I'll write when the energy hits, but by the time the kids are in bed and the house is quiet, I'm done." She's not alone.

Research supports this experience. A comprehensive meta-analysis by Gollwitzer and Sheeran (2006) found that forming implementation intentions—specific "if-then" plans that link situational cues to goal-directed behaviors—significantly increased the likelihood of goal attainment across various domains. The effect size was medium to large (d = 0.65), indicating a robust impact on translating intentions into action.[47]

Because here's the truth: Motivation doesn't create momentum. Momentum creates motivation. If you want to be consistent, you need a plan that works even on your worst days, not just your best ones. You need actions that don't require a perfect mood or a burst of inspiration. You need a process that says, "No matter how I feel, this is what I do." It might not feel exciting. It might not even feel productive in the moment. But over time, those boring, imperfect, unglamorous actions are what move the needle the most, so if you've been stuck waiting for the right energy to strike, stop waiting. Start small, show up anyway, and let the doing be what creates the feeling.

# Build a System That Builds You Back

Now that we've talked about why consistency breaks down, let's talk about how to build it back up on your terms. Not by relying on more motivation, not by expecting yourself to wake up at 5:00 AM and suddenly become someone you're not, but by creating habits that align with the life you actually live, and then staying accountable to them through regular check-ins that honor your season, your energy, and your values.

The truth is, consistency isn't about doing the same thing every day perfectly. It's about creating systems that make it easier for you to show up, even when life gets chaotic. It's about reducing friction and building rituals that keep you moving forward, even when your goals evolve.

Let's start with the habits themselves, and then we'll talk about how to stay accountable to them using a system that works in every season.

*Exercise*

## Build the Habit

One of the most common questions I get from coaching clients, workshop attendees, and even friends is: "How do I make this new habit stick?" They're often surprised when I tell them they're asking the wrong question.

Habits don't stick because you try harder. They stick because you design your environment, your expectations, and your energy around them. And they evolve when you evolve. Like many lessons in this book, this is one I learned firsthand—the hard way.

I was terrified when I first decided I was ready to start dating again, not of dating, exactly, but of what it might reveal about me. I agonized: *Would I be able to trust someone again? Would I fall back into old patterns? Would I get distracted from my work or let myself be mistreated again?*

The only way I was going to find out was to take action, so I did what I now coach hundreds of women to do when they're ready to start a new chapter: I created a system. I didn't just download the apps and wing it. I approached it like I would a project at work—strategically, intentionally, and with a plan to refine as I went.

Here's the exact process I used—and still use—with clients to build meaningful habits that actually last:

## Step 1: **Pick the Habit**

This seems obvious but it's worth saying. You have to start with one habit—not five. And it has to be clear. Not "get back out there" or "be healthier," but something tangible and specific. In my case, it was "I'm going to start dating again."

## Step 2: **Set the Anchor**

When exactly are you going to do it? Where will you be? What will prompt it? Habits need anchors. I decided I'd check dating apps each evening after dinner and hold Thursday nights open for dates. My au pair worked late those evenings, so I built around that existing support.

## Step 3: **Identify Roadblocks**

Where will this fall apart? Be honest. I knew that by the end of the day, I'd be mentally tapped and likely to forget, so I set a daily reminder on my phone. That small nudge made it harder to skip and easier to start.

## *Step 4:* **Test It**

Habits are experiments, not declarations. I started the routine and used my daily Recap Ritual (more on that shortly) to note how it was going. I even kept detailed notes on each date just five minutes after getting home so I wouldn't forget names, stories, or red flags.

## *Step 5:* **Reassess After Thirty Days**

After a month of dating, I looked at what was working and what wasn't. By that point, I had adjusted the process, refined my preferences, and begun forming connections. The habit had become part of my rhythm.

## *Step 6:* **Sustain or Shift**

Eventually, I met someone I wanted to focus on exclusively, so I shifted the habit—less time on apps, more time deepening that connection. That habit evolved as my goals did. And that's what made it sustainable.

What's most important here is not that you follow this framework perfectly but that you remember one thing: You're not building a habit for the sake of the habit. You're building a habit that reflects the life you want—and the person you're becoming.

James Clear refers to this as building "identity-based habits" in his book *Atomic Habits.* You don't build the habit of writing just to write. You build the habit because you're becoming someone who communicates clearly, documents their journey, or brings ideas into the world. You don't just work out to lose weight. You do it because you're becoming someone who honors their body and prioritizes their energy. I didn't just build the habit of dating so I could stoke my ego and feel good about myself. I did it because I was becoming the future partner of a man willing to put in the same level of effort and who therefore was truly deserving of both me and my son.

Every habit you build is a vote for your future self: not just the one you want to become, but the one who's already waiting inside you, ready to be let out.

For some of my clients, building consistency also means building infrastructure—tools like checklists, dashboards, templates, and automation that reduce decision fatigue and keep them focused on keeping up with their habits. If you're juggling a demanding job, a household, and a big vision, don't be afraid to use tools that support you. Systems aren't a crutch. They're a strategy.

Once the habit is in place, though, the real challenge—keeping it going—begins. That's where the Recap Ritual comes in.

## Stay Accountable with the Recap Ritual

This is the system I use every single day, week, month, quarter, and year, not just to stay on track, but to *redefine the track as needed*. Because if there's one thing I've learned, it's that consistency doesn't mean doing the same thing forever. It means showing up for your life on purpose, again and again, even when the terrain changes.

The Recap Ritual is simple. It involves asking yourself three questions at regular intervals:

1. What went well today/this week/this month/this quarter/this year?
2. What didn't go well?
3. What will I do differently moving forward?

That's it—no complex spreadsheet and no app required—just reflection, honesty, and course correction.

What makes this powerful is not the questions themselves but the *cadence*. Here's how I recommend you use it:

- **Daily:** Set aside five minutes at the end of your workday for a quick check-in to stay grounded.
- **Weekly:** Plan to take one hour on a Friday or Sunday to review wins, missed steps, and reset your priorities.
- **Monthly:** Take two hours to look at patterns and ask yourself: Where are you trending? What deserves more focus?
- **Quarterly:** Schedule three hours to zoom out and reconnect to the big picture.
- **Annually:** Take a full day to reflect, celebrate, and envision what's next.

Some of my clients do this in a digital Notion dashboard (like I do). Others use paper journals, audio voice notes, or even color-coded whiteboards, but the method doesn't matter. What matters is that you *make time* to reflect—on purpose—not just when you crash.

These rituals help you build self-trust. They prevent you from abandoning goals just because you hit a bump. They also allow you to see when a goal needs to evolve because your season, your values, or your capacity has changed. You'll be amazed how many decisions get easier once you're regularly checking in with your own data, your own needs, and your own results.

## Putting It All Together

# Consistency Isn't About Perfection; It's About Self-Leadership

If you've made it this far in the book, there are a few things I know for sure about you: You're not lazy. You're not broken. You're not unmotivated. You're just overwhelmed, and no one ever taught you how to build systems that work for your life as it actually is. That's what the Lack of Consistency Overwhelm Culprit is all about.

You start with good intentions. You set the goals. You buy the planner. You even get off to a strong start. But then life does what it always does, it throws curveballs, distractions, competing priorities, exhaustion in your way. And suddenly, the progress you were making slips through your fingers—*again*. This isn't because you're incapable. It's because your consistency was built on hope, not infrastructure.

You've been trying to stay consistent using willpower alone, without a structure to support you on the hard days. You've been stuck in stop–start cycles, overcommitting out of guilt or people-pleasing, and then collapsing when you inevitably run out of energy. You've relied on external accountability—deadlines, pressure, the expectations of others—to move forward instead of building the internal systems that make forward motion sustainable. And you're tired—not just physically tired, but tired of not trusting yourself to follow through, tired of making promises to yourself and breaking them, tired of wondering if you'll ever be able to create real momentum without burning out in the process. When you learn how to lead yourself consistently, everything else changes; that's why this chapter matters so much.

The tools I've shared with you in this chapter are the same tools I've used to rebuild my own life—starting with small habits and simple reflections that helped me take aligned action, even when I didn't feel like it.

You've learned how to create meaningful, realistic habits with the Custom Habit Builder, a six-step framework to help you anchor new behaviors into your actual schedule and identify roadblocks before they derail your progress.

You've also learned how to stay accountable to those habits using the Recap Ritual, a self-leadership practice that creates built-in reflection at regular intervals so you can notice what's working, what's not, and what needs to shift. It's not just about tracking your progress, it's about honoring your capacity, noticing your growth, and leading yourself through the messy middle.

And here's the truth: Consistency isn't rigid. It's responsive. It adapts to the season you're in. That's exactly what I had to learn when I decided I was ready to date again after years of living alone in survival mode. I created a simple daily habit of checking my dating apps after dinner and tracking my conversations, and a weekly habit of holding Thursday evenings open for first dates. I used my Recap Ritual to reflect on what I was learning, how I was showing up, and what I needed to adjust along with my other priorities. That one habit, done consistently over the course of a year, changed everything.

I dated over fifty men in that time. Not because I was desperate, but because I was committed. I wasn't looking for a fantasy. I was building clarity. I was not only learning how to trust myself again, I was also discovering exactly what it was I was looking for in my next relationship. I was practicing setting boundaries, noticing patterns, and healing the parts of me that still wanted to shrink or settle.

And then, I met Franco.

Franco was the first person who made me feel safe enough to be fully seen. With him, I could soften. I could ask for what I needed. I could lead without hiding behind control. His presence changed me, not because he "fixed" me, but because he reflected back the version of me I had worked so hard to reclaim.

Losing him shattered me. There's no other way to say it. When he died, I lost not just the man I loved, but the version of myself I had become through that relationship. Grief stripped me down to the studs, and for a while, I didn't know if I could rebuild again. But I had something I didn't have before. I had tools. I had systems. I had rituals. I had a framework, and even though I was broken open, I was not broken beyond repair.

In the next section, I'll show you how I led myself through that season—not by trying to "move on," but by using everything I had taught and lived to stay in motion through the darkest time of my life. I'll show you how I applied the Five Overwhelm Culprits step-by-step in the middle of real, relentless grief. And I'll show you what happened next—not just how I found love again, but how I found myself again.

That's the real power of consistency: It doesn't just keep you moving forward when things are going well, it anchors you when everything falls apart.

*Part Four*

# Relentless Resilience

# Chapter Ten

# Leading Yourself Through the Hardest Times

*To the victim, adversity is bad.*
*To the leader and warrior, hard times are life's richest*
*times of growth, opportunity and possibility.*
*Use them to fly.*
—Robin Sharma

My eyes, swollen from crying, fluttered open in the morning. Light pierced through the curtains like a spotlight I didn't ask for. I was buried under a mountain of blankets, the weight of them both a comfort and a trap despite the August heat.

Out of habit, I reached for my phone. It was a reflex, a way to check the time, and more instinctively, to read the good morning message Franco sent me every single day.

The screen flashed 8:00 AM.

There was no message.

Right. *Franco can't message me anymore. Franco is dead.*

My stomach dropped. The shock, somehow, still felt new. It had been over six weeks since his suicide and yet, every single morning, I'd wake up hoping I'd imagined it all; that this would be the day I'd open my eyes and find it was just a dream.

From the other room, I heard my son giggle. "Cake cakes!" he says, asking for more pancakes. *He must be having breakfast with our au pair.*

The sound of his joy pierces me with guilt.

He's been up since six. *"What kind of mother sleeps through her son waking up? I didn't even get out of bed in time to feed him. What kind of example is that?"* The shame hit like a second wave. My eyes sting again, and I stare at the ceiling, blinking through tears. I'd cried so much the past few weeks that I'd given myself a sinus infection and landed in urgent care for an antibiotic. My grief had literally made me sick.

Still, I remember the intention I'd set for myself the night before: I would not get out of bed until I had thought of three things I was grateful for, no matter how small, no matter how forced, and no matter how much it hurt. It was a beautiful idea when I wrote it down but much harder to implement in the here and now when the man you love has taken his own life, when you were the one to find him. When you're so traumatized you can't work, you can't show up for your child. You can barely show up for yourself. How do you find gratitude when everything around you feels scorched and gray?

Another giggle from the kitchen, my son, my sweet boy. He is my everything. If not for him, I might still be stuck in the abusive relationship I fought so hard to escape. In many ways, he saved me. That's *one.*

I hear the au pair offering him more syrup. "Dip dip?" she asks. Her calm, loving presence over the last six weeks has been the safety net I didn't know I'd need. Between her and my mother, my son has been cared for when I couldn't. For that, I am profoundly grateful. That's *two*.

I glance across the room and see my laundry hamper—empty. Yesterday, I finally washed a few weeks' worth of dirty clothes that I'd been avoiding. It's a small thing. But it counts. No laundry today. *Three*.

It's enough to move.

I slowly peeled back the covers and sat up. I had used my Recap Ritual the night before to outline what needed my attention today. Small things, manageable things—eat, journal, go to therapy, try to get outside, stay connected—things I couldn't always manage to do but things I was determined to try again.

While I was still clear on my overall vision of what I wanted from this life and the kind of leader I wanted to be, losing the person I thought would be part of that vision had left me gutted. I could barely care for my son. I could barely breathe some days. But I knew I had to find a way to rebuild, piece by piece.

Therapy with Elizabeth had become a lifeline. That day, I had another appointment, along with some journaling homework she'd assigned. It was a start.

The loneliness, though, was harder to fix. In the months leading up to Franco's death, I'd started to feel distant from the single mom friends who once surrounded me. Maybe because I'd been in a relationship? Maybe because they didn't know how to hold grief? They didn't come to the funeral. They didn't call after. And that absence cut deep.

I knew I needed community. So, I did what I always do when I feel lost—I made a plan. I started researching local suicide loss support groups and found one close by that met on Tuesday nights. I decided I would go. I would try. But first, I needed to eat.

The trauma had stripped ten pounds off my already lean frame. A group of Franco's friends who had once done Whole30 with us had reached out. They were doing another round, in his honor, and invited me to join. I agreed—not because I had the energy, but because I needed the structure. I had meal prepped over the weekend so I wouldn't have to think. I could just grab and eat, a small win.

And then, there was movement, fresh air, and sunshine. I'd noticed how much better I felt—physically, emotionally—when I made it to the beach or took a short walk. I couldn't always do it, but I knew it helped when I did.

The truth was, I was starting and stopping a lot. The discord was compounded by the stress of returning to my twenty-hour weekly commute on the days I attempted to go to the office. Most days I'd get there and have a panic attack in the bathroom before having to return to my desk like nothing was wrong. Some days I could eat. Other days I couldn't. Some days I could walk. Other days, I couldn't leave the bed. I wasn't showing up for my son the way I wanted, and I definitely wasn't showing up for myself. I couldn't.

I had to let go of the pressure to be perfect, and I made a new rule: I would take it day by day. And every day, I would begin with three things I was grateful for—no matter how small, no matter how strained. That was the first step. And I didn't know it at the time, but it was also the beginning of something else: a system, a structure, a self-leadership strategy built entirely around the Overwhelm Culprits.

In that moment, I wasn't thinking about the "framework." I was just surviving. But the truth is, I was already putting the work into action. I was rebuilding community. I was supporting my conditioning. I was anchoring new consistency.

In this chapter, I'll show you how I did it on purpose. Because if you're reading this, there's a good chance you've been through your own breaking point, the kind of moment you don't bounce back from, the kind you *build back* from slowly, intentionally, with help.

This chapter is for those moments, the ones that strip you bare and force you to start again. And I'm here to walk you through it.

## When Everything Falls Apart, Self-Leadership Begins

There are seasons in life when no planner, no affirmation, no amount of caffeine can get you through the day. These are the seasons when grief, trauma, or profound change knocks you off your feet, and no matter how high-functioning you've been in the past, you find yourself staring at the ceiling wondering how you'll make it through the next hour, let alone the next year.

It's not that you don't want to keep going. It's that everything in you is screaming to *stop*. And when you're a woman who's built your identity on being the strong one—the reliable one, the high achiever, the caretaker—this collapse doesn't just feel like a crisis. It feels like a failure, like you've broken some unspoken contract with the world that says you're not allowed to fall apart.

But know this: Falling apart isn't failure; it's feedback, it's your body, your mind, and your soul telling you that the life you were living before no longer fits the reality you're living in now.

This chapter is not about bouncing back. It's about rebuilding slowly, intentionally, with structure, with grace, and with a new kind of leadership—one that starts from the inside out.

Before we can talk about strategy, we have to name what's happening.

If you've ever felt like you're drowning in a moment that changed everything, you're not alone. And you're not broken.

Let's talk about why this feels so hard—and what's really going on underneath the surface.

# I Can't Think Clearly or Take Action

One of the first casualties of personal crisis is your ability to think clearly and take purposeful action. Even simple tasks—like deciding what to eat, responding to a text, or getting out of bed—can feel insurmountable. This isn't a reflection of your character or motivation; it's a manifestation of your brain's response to trauma.

When faced with significant stress or trauma, the brain's prefrontal cortex, responsible for decision-making and rational thought, can become underactive. Simultaneously, the amygdala, which governs our fight-or-flight responses, becomes overactive. This shift prioritizes immediate survival over complex cognitive functions, leading to what's often described as "brain fog" or executive dysfunction. Research supports these observations. A study published in the *Journal of Traumatic Stress* found that individuals who experienced trauma in adulthood exhibited greater cognitive decline, particularly in areas related to executive function, compared to those without such experiences.[48] Additionally, grief has been shown to impair executive functions, affecting one's ability to plan, focus, and regulate emotions.

Understanding that these cognitive challenges are rooted in physiological changes can be liberating. It shifts the narrative from self-blame to self-compassion. Recognizing that your brain is in survival mode allows you to adjust expectations and strategies accordingly.

This is why simple systems matter. When your brain can't carry the weight, structure can. Things like preparing meals in advance, predeciding your schedule, or limiting choices can help reduce cognitive overload. These aren't productivity hacks, they're survival scaffolding. And when you're rebuilding from a breaking point, that scaffolding can be the difference between staying stuck and taking a single, sustainable step forward.

# I Feel Like Everything Is Falling Apart and It's My Fault

When life collapses—a loss hits, a relationship ends, or everything you've been holding together suddenly breaks—it's easy to feel like you've failed.

You look around at the mess—the unread emails, the unwashed dishes, the missed deadlines, the meals you didn't make, the child you couldn't comfort—and instead of seeing those things as symptoms of trauma, you start seeing them as proof: proof that you're not good enough, proof that you're not strong enough, or proof that *you're* the problem.

This guilt doesn't come out of nowhere. It's inherited, reinforced, and rewarded. Most high-performing women are raised to believe that their value comes from being competent, composed, and in control at all times. We are praised for our independence, our emotional labor, our ability to manage everyone else's needs without letting our own show. And when we do it well, we're seen as reliable, responsible, resilient.

But what happens when we can't?

What happens when the thing we couldn't control—grief, illness, divorce, burnout, death—brings our carefully constructed lives crashing down? We don't just grieve the loss. We grieve losing the version of ourselves who *could* handle it all. And instead of extending ourselves the same grace we offer others, we self-punish.

There's a deeper reason for this pattern. Research has shown that women are more likely than men to develop internalizing disorders such as anxiety, depression, and post-traumatic stress following trauma. According to the U.S. Department of Veterans Affairs, this tendency to turn distress inward is not only more common in women but also contributes to a higher prevalence of PTSD among women than men, even though men are more likely to experience trauma overall.[49]

In other words, when women face traumatic events, they're more likely to internalize the pain and blame themselves for the fallout. And because no one sees it, this internal collapse is often more painful than the external one. Because, deep down, you thought that if you could just keep everything together, you'd be safe: You wouldn't be vulnerable; you wouldn't be the one who needed saving. But here's the truth: The house was already on fire. You were just too busy trying to hold up the walls to smell the smoke.

Your overwhelm is not a failure. It's a sign. It's pointing you toward something that needs to be seen, softened, and ultimately healed, not punished.

This chapter is not about making you feel better for falling apart. It's about giving you the tools to stop blaming yourself for something that was never yours to carry alone.

## I Don't Know What to Do Next

There comes a point in every breakdown when the urgency fades, the initial shock wears off, and you're just . . . suspended, not moving, not planning, not recovering. You want to take action, but every direction feels equally unclear. Every to-do list feels irrelevant. Every next step feels either overwhelming or pointless. This is one of the most terrifying parts of personal crisis: not the chaos itself, but the stillness that follows, that eerie, frozen silence where you can no longer access your instincts, your drive, or your confidence.

And if you're someone who's usually on top of everything—your work, your calendar, your goals—this disorientation hits even harder. You're used to being able to strategize your way through hard things, so when your brain fails to offer up a clear next move, it feels like the most unforgivable betrayal. This is not a failure of intelligence. It's a failure of focus. You're not broken, you're just trying to solve the wrong problem.

When everything in your life feels out of alignment, it's not because you don't care. It's because you haven't yet identified what's actually driving the overwhelm.

Are you burned out from doing too much without support?

Are you disconnected from your long-term vision?

Are you lacking confidence, clarity, or even the energy to make a plan?

You don't need a productivity hack. You need a diagnostic tool. That's exactly why I developed the Overwhelm Culprits framework. When I was in the depths of my own grief—confused, exhausted, and desperate for direction—I realized that the chaos I was experiencing wasn't random. It was a pattern, and it was trying to tell me something. Once I identified the specific Culprits contributing to my overwhelm, I stopped spinning and started taking aligned, strategic action—one small step at a time.

If you're stuck right now and unsure what to do next, don't try to force clarity; instead, ask yourself a different question: *Which Overwhelm Culprit is driving this season of overwhelm?*

In the next section, I'll walk you through exactly how I used that lens to rebuild during one of the most painful chapters of my life. And if you're not sure where to start, I created a free quiz you can access at www.corrielo.com/overwhelmculprit that can help you identify your current Culprit and take your next step with more confidence.

You don't need to figure it all out. You just need to figure out where to begin.

## I Know What I Should Do, but I Can't Follow Through

You've done the work. You've named your Culprit. You've made the plan. You even feel moments of clarity—of vision—like maybe you're ready to move. And then . . . nothing happens. You freeze. You doomscroll. You spiral. You shut down. Then you shame yourself for shutting down.

This isn't indecision; you've already decided. This isn't confusion; you're actually clear. It's your nervous system putting the brakes on because it doesn't feel safe to act—even on the things you *want* to do. This is a trauma response called functional freeze, which occurs when your executive functioning is online enough to know what should happen but your body stays locked in stillness.[50] It's like being trapped behind glass, watching your life unfold without the strength to participate in it.

Not all freeze responses look like immobility. Sometimes, you're still going through the motions while emotionally frozen inside. This kind of freeze is devastating for high-functioning women. It creates a double wound: first, the wound of whatever you've been through and second, the internal narrative that you're lazy, broken, or not trying hard enough. But what if you're not broken? What if freeze isn't a failure but a flag, a sign that you've moved too fast, pushed too hard, or tried to perform healing instead of allowing it?

Research indicates that trauma can impair executive functions such as planning, decision-making, and task execution. A study published in *Neuropsychopharmacology* highlights how trauma-related changes in the prefrontal cortex can affect goal-directed behavior, leading to difficulties in initiating and completing tasks.[51] Which can explain why even brushing your teeth or returning a text feels like climbing a mountain.

Understanding that this response is rooted in neurobiology, not personal inadequacy, can be the first step toward self-compassion and healing.

# I Can't Stay Positive No Matter How Hard I Try

There's a particular kind of pressure that shows up in crisis: the pressure to be okay. You may be grieving, exhausted, completely lost, but still, there's that internal voice whispering: *"Come on. You should be grateful." "Other people have it worse." "You're supposed to be strong." "He's in a better place now."*

Maybe that voice isn't even yours. Maybe it came from childhood or from the workplace. Or from the endless parade of inspirational quotes telling you to "choose joy" or "trust the process."

Yet, when you try to find something to be positive about—anything—it feels forced, hollow. You know you should feel thankful for what you still have, but your system is so depleted it just feels like another thing you're failing at.

This is what happens when a high-functioning woman reaches her limit. The mindset tools that used to work—reframing, gratitude, optimism—don't land the same way. This is not because you're ungrateful but because your nervous system is in survival mode. When your body is still trying to process grief, shock, or loss, reaching for positivity can feel impossible.

It's not that you don't want to feel better. It's that you're biologically, emotionally, and mentally maxed out. And if you've built your identity on being the strong one—the one who always bounces back—this breakdown of positivity doesn't just feel hard, it feels like a threat to who you *are*.

That's why this chapter doesn't ask you to "look on the bright side." Instead, it asks  different questions: *What if you didn't need to be positive right now? What if you just needed to stay present—and grounded—long enough to start healing?*

In the next section, I'll walk you through how I did that for myself—through the tools that helped me anchor into something real, even when everything else felt lost.

I discovered that you don't need a positive attitude to move forward, you just need a clear starting point . . . and a little space to breathe.

## Rebuilding from the Inside Out

When everything falls apart, the instinct is often to try to put it all back together exactly as it was. You want your energy back. Your confidence back. Your future back. But in the wake of deep trauma, that kind of return isn't possible, at least not right away. And often, trying to force it only leaves you more depleted, more disconnected, and even more overwhelmed. That was certainly true for me.

Over a five-year period, I endured what most people experience over a lifetime: relationship trauma, divorce, single parenting, suicide loss, rebuilding my identity. There were seasons I couldn't breathe, let alone build, yet I did rebuild, slowly, not by pushing harder, but by leading myself with grace, strategy, and small consistent tools that created capacity again, piece by piece.

That's what this section is about. It's not about "fixing" what happened. It's about supporting yourself through it, using practices that are flexible, trauma informed, and empowering even when you feel at your lowest.

Here are the three core strategies that helped me move from barely functioning to grounded momentum.

# Shift from a Five-Year Vision to a Day-by-Day Vision

If you've been with me since Chapter 4, you already know how powerful a Five-Year Vision can be. Most high-performing women naturally think this way. It's how we plan, how we build, how we dream. But when you're in the middle of trauma, your brain simply isn't capable of that kind of long-range thinking. Neuroscience tells us that when your nervous system is in survival mode, your pre-frontal cortex—the part of your brain responsible for future planning and rational decision-making—goes quiet. Instead, your mind is focused on one thing: making it through today.

Trying to push a long-term vision when your body is still in crisis doesn't build clarity, it builds shame. And that's not what you need right now. That's why one of the most healing shifts I made during my own grief was this: I stopped thinking in years and started thinking in *days*. Instead of asking, *Where do I want to be in five years?* I asked, *What does my ideal day look like*—today? What would it look like to support my nervous system, to feel grounded instead of overwhelmed, to feel proud for just showing up?

This daily question became the foundation of my healing, and it aligned beautifully with the daily layer of my Recap Ritual—**a practice I still use today.**

Each evening, I'd take five minutes to reflect on:

1. What went well today?
2. What didn't go well?
3. What will I do differently tomorrow?

That was it: Just reflecting on the day in front of me, not the week, the month, or the year.

Eventually, as I began to heal, I found myself naturally gravitating toward my weekly and monthly Recap Rituals again. And eventually, even my Five-Year Vision came back. It didn't feel like pressure. It felt like possibility.

If you're in a hard season right now, I want to give you permission to press pause on the big picture. You don't need a master plan. You just need a compass. And sometimes, that compass only points one day ahead at a time.

Alternatively, if you're reading this and thinking, *Damn, my problems are not anywhere near as serious as what Corrie went through,* you may not need the information in this section, or even this chapter, right now. But you can rest easy that one day, if that hard season hits—because pivotal life moments affect everyone at some point in time—you'll know exactly how to shift from the Five-Year Vision mindset to the "let's just get through the day" one and guide yourself through it with clarity, confidence, and grace.

## Start a Daily Gratitude Practice

In the depths of my grief, when everything felt heavy and hope seemed distant, I stumbled upon a simple practice that became a lifeline: Before getting out of bed each morning, I identified three things I was grateful for. Initially, these weren't grand revelations. They were small, tangible acknowledgments:

- "I'm grateful I did the laundry yesterday."
- "I'm thankful I found my son's missing shoe."
- "I'm appreciative of the quiet moment I had with my coffee."

This daily ritual wasn't about dismissing my pain but about creating space for moments of relief amidst the chaos. Over time, this practice rewired my focus. I began to notice and seek out these positive moments throughout my day, which gradually shifted my perspective from one of despair to one of resilience.

Scientific research supports the efficacy of such gratitude practices. A meta-analysis of sixty-four randomized clinical trials found that participants who engaged in gratitude interventions experienced significant improvements in mental health, including reduced symptoms of anxiety and depression, and increased life satisfaction.[52]

Moreover, a study published in *Psychotherapy Research* demonstrated that clients who wrote gratitude letters reported better mental health outcomes compared to those who didn't engage in such writing.[53] These findings highlight that even simple acts of gratitude can have profound effects on your mental well-being if you take the time to look for them.

Even now, I continue this practice as part of my daily journaling. It's a small, consistent action that helps me stay grounded, fosters resilience, and reminds me that there are always moments worth appreciating amidst the challenges.

## Use the Overwhelm Culprit Cycle

Finally, when I looked back at those times when everything felt like too much and I didn't know where to start, I recognized that what had helped me get unstuck was the Overwhelm Culprit Cycle. After identifying all the patterns between what helped me lead myself personally and professionally following the trauma of my high-conflict divorce and applying it to my post-suicide loss situation, I observed that feelings of overwhelm flow in a cycle. This is the process I now teach my clients, my audiences, and my team because it's simple, intuitive, and repeatable for life.

Here's how it works:

1. You feel overwhelmed.
2. You identify your current Overwhelm Culprit, either by using the quiz at www.corrielo.com/overwhelmculprit or by scanning the five Culprit types we covered earlier in the book.
3. You apply the tools from that Culprit's chapter to make small, consistent changes that support that specific need.
4. You make strategic progress aligned with your current capacity.
5. You continue forward until life shifts again and you come back to the cycle, starting fresh.

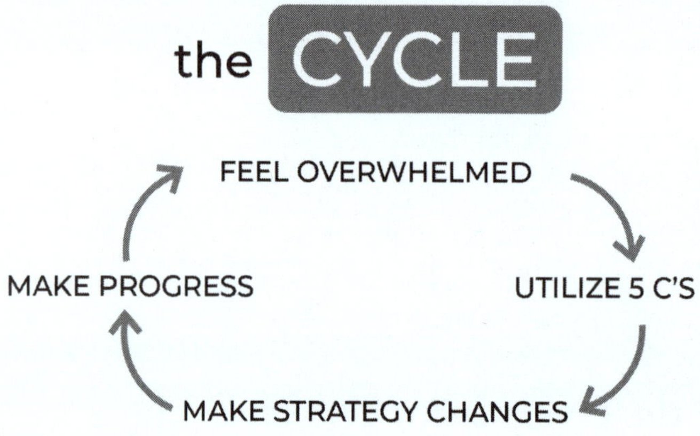


Take my situation at the beginning of this chapter as an example. It was obvious that I was dealing with three of the five culprits at that time. I still had clarity. I knew exactly what I wanted and was crystal clear on my desired Five-Year Vision, which is why losing my partner in life who was supposed to join me for it was that much more painful. I also was extremely confident. I had Franco to help for rebuilding that in me.

However, the things I was struggling with included losing my core social group and once again not having people around me who understood the complexity of suicide loss. Those struggles also included the rapid decline of both my physical and mental health due to the trauma. Lastly, I was finding it nearly impossible to be consistent with anything in life personally or professionally, especially with the incredible stress I was already under pre-suicide loss with my twenty-hour weekly commute. Knowing this, it was easier to implement small, incremental changes.

I signed up for the suicide loss support group. I meal prepped and started Whole30 again so I'd eat healthfully. I started my gratitude practice and kept up with my weekly therapy sessions. I still had to figure out what to do about my commute and how to become more consistent again, but at least I felt in control regarding the other areas of my life during a time when life felt completely out of control.

What makes this so powerful is that the Culprit that's showing up today may not be the same one you were struggling with last month. I've had people attend the same keynote at two different events and come up to me afterward saying they walked away with two completely different breakthroughs—just because their current Culprit had changed.

The goal isn't perfection. It's momentum. The more you know how to self-diagnose your overwhelm and respond with targeted tools, the faster you propel forward.

## Putting It All Together

# Small, Daily Actions Compound over Time

When you're in the middle of trauma, loss, or a total life collapse, it's easy to feel like you've failed, that you've lost your edge, your energy, and your ability to lead. But what's actually happening is deeper—and far more human. Your nervous system is doing everything it can to protect you. Your brain is conserving energy for survival. And the high-functioning habits that once made you feel strong are now being filtered through a completely different set of physical, emotional, and mental lenses.

In this chapter, we named the five most common breakdown points women experience when they're overwhelmed by crisis:

1. You can't think clearly or take action—because your brain is in survival mode, not strategy mode.
2. You feel like everything is falling apart and it's your fault—because women are socially conditioned to internalize stress and blame.
3. You don't know what to do next—because you haven't yet identified the true source of your overwhelm.
4. You know what to do but can't follow through—because functional freeze keeps your body from executing what your brain already understands.
5. You can't stay positive—because false positivity isn't healing, and your nervous system is already maxed out.

From there, I introduced three tools that helped me rebuild from some of the hardest experiences of my life:

- **Shifting from a Five-Year Vision to a day-by-day vision,** supported by a daily Recap Ritual to gently regain focus and momentum without overwhelm
- **Practicing daily gratitude,** not to force positivity, but to retrain your mind to notice what's still working—even in the middle of deep grief
- **Using the Overwhelm Culprit Cycle** to self-diagnose and take aligned, strategic action whenever you feel stuck, so you can regain momentum and move forward on your own terms

These aren't hacks, they're anchors. They help you lead yourself back to solid ground—one moment, one breath, one choice at a time.

# A Note on Mental Health Support

I want to be clear about something important: I didn't do this alone. While the tools and frameworks in this book were essential, I would never have made the progress I did without the support of Elizabeth, my therapist. Healing from trauma is hard work, and one of the most powerful decisions I made was asking for help getting through the abuse, the divorce, and the suicide loss.

I am not a licensed mental health professional. I am someone who is deeply trauma informed through lived experience, coaching, and ongoing study. The practices shared in this book are meant to support your healing, not replace clinical care.

If you are currently navigating trauma, grief, depression, anxiety, or loss, I strongly encourage you to seek the support of a licensed therapist or counselor alongside this work. You deserve care that is as deep as the pain you've been carrying.

*Exercise*

# How to Find the Right Therapist

One of the most common questions I get is, *"How do I find a good therapist?"* My honest answer: **You try more than one.** Finding the right therapist is a lot like dating. You are allowed to interview, ask questions, and walk away if it doesn't feel right. You can respect someone's credentials and still recognize they are not *your* person.

Here is a simple process that works.

### *Step 1:* **Start with what you need right now.**

You do not need the perfect label for your experience. Just start with your best guess:

- Trauma or PTSD
- Grief and loss
- Anxiety or panic
- Depression
- Relationship recovery
- Couples and family
- Stress, overwhelm, and burnout
- Life transitions

If you're not sure, that's okay. A good clinician will help you clarify as you go.

## *Step 2:* **Use trusted places to search.**

These directories are widely used and are a solid starting point:

- Psychology Today Therapist Directory: https://www.psychologytoday.com/us/therapists
- TherapyDen: https://www.therapyden.com
- GoodTherapy: https://www.goodtherapy.org
- Open Path Collective (lower-cost therapy): https://openpathcollective.org
- If you have insurance, search your provider's "Find a Provider" tool (often the most cost-effective route)

If you prefer to work with someone trained in trauma, you can also search specifically for trauma modalities such as EMDR.

- EMDR International Association directory: https://www.emdria.org/find-an-emdr-therapist/

## *Step 3:* **Interview a few therapists before you commit.**

Most therapists will offer a brief consultation call or intake conversation. You're not being difficult—you're being discerning.

Helpful questions to ask:

- What is your experience working with trauma and grief?
- What modalities do you use (and what does that look like in sessions)?
- What does progress typically look like with the type of challenges I'm navigating?
- What should I expect in the first month of working together?

*Step 4:* **Choose safety over politeness.**

Therapy only works when you feel safe enough to be honest.

Green flags:

- You feel seen, not judged.
- You leave feeling supported—even if you were challenged.
- You feel comfortable being truthful.
- You trust their pacing and guidance.

Red flags:

- You feel dismissed, rushed, or talked over.
- You leave feeling ashamed or unsafe.
- You feel pressure to share more than you're ready to shar.e
- Your boundaries are minimized.

If it's not a fit, you are allowed to switch. That is not failure; that is you advocating for your healing.

## If You Need Help Right Now

If you are in immediate danger, call your local emergency number.

If you are in the United States:

- 988 Suicide & Crisis Lifeline: Call or text 988: https://988lifeline.org
- Crisis Text Line: Text HOME to 741741: https://www.crisistextline.org

If you are outside the United States, you can find local crisis resources here:

- International crisis hotline directory:
  https://www.opencounseling.com/suicide-hotlines

Getting help is not a weakness. It is leadership. And if no one has told you this yet, let me be clear: You are allowed to receive support. You do not have to earn it.

But what happens when you're back on your feet . . . and still not getting different results? What happens when you're doing the work, taking action, checking the boxes, and nothing's changing? That's exactly what we're going to explore next.

In the next chapter, we're going to talk about why high performers fear change, how to shift when your current strategy is no longer working, and how to redefine failure as the most valuable leadership data you'll ever collect.

Let's keep going.

# Chapter Eleven

# Become a Professional Failure

*Giving up is the only sure way to fail.*
—Gena Showalter

I didn't know it yet, but this night would mark the first time I truly embraced one of the hardest lessons of my life: If you want a different result, you have to try a different approach.

## New Year's Eve, 2018

I was absolutely mortified.

It was almost six months to the day since Franco's death. My toddler was asleep. I was wide-awake and alone, trying desperately not to spiral as memories of the New Year's Eve we spent together the year before hit me like a freight train. On that New Year's Eve, we'd toasted to our goals and dreams for the year ahead, goals and dreams that would never come to pass.

To distract myself, I sat at my kitchen table, cutting out print-outs of Pinterest images for a new vision board. Each image made me whisper silently, *Yes, universe: that, please* as I scrolled through images of couples holding hands, embracing on beaches, a replacement for my ugly sofa, and quotes that struck a nerve. Dreams of becoming a professional speaker and an author—a new version of me—felt light-years away.

I was so focused, I didn't even realize the Times Square ball had dropped. My phone rang, and in my distracted haze, I answered a FaceTime call without checking who it was. Suddenly, my tear-streaked, mascara-smeared face filled the screen and I was face-to-face with my parents and all their friends celebrating the New Year in Florida.

Before they could even shout *Happy New Year, sweetheart!* I was bawling, overcome by the thought, *How can anyone celebrate? I just need this piece-of-shit year to end.*

I was crying so hard I don't even remember the rest of the call, just the humiliation of breaking down in front of a crowd of well-meaning strangers, the kind of loneliness that chokes you from the inside out, and the realization that no matter how hard I tried to rebuild, I kept ending up in the same place.

That night, I cried myself to sleep with my vision board soaked in sauvignon blanc and tears.

## New Year's Day, 2019

The next morning, I woke up . . . weirdly grateful, grateful that 2018 was finally over, grateful that I'd survived the horror of broadcasting my breakdown to my parents' entire New Year's Eve party, and grateful I had the day off from work to recover.

My son and I spent the morning snuggling on the couch, watching cartoons. Something about that moment reminded me of how much I missed sharing these moments—with Franco, with someone. I hadn't even *considered* dating again. But that morning, one thought wouldn't leave me alone: *You can't keep doing the same thing and expect a different result.*

Over the last six months, I'd clawed my way back to a life that was finally starting to feel okay. And now, those moments that once brought me joy were making me ache with loneliness.

If I wanted to share this life with someone again, I had to try something different, even if it scared the hell out of me. My last two relationships had left me traumatized—one literally, one in ways I'm still unpacking. But the images on my vision board said it was possible to love again, so I asked myself: *What's worse: staying single as a divorcee and pseudo widow, heart shielded forever, or taking the risk that maybe, just maybe, I could find love again?*

The *Mickey Mouse Clubhouse* blared from the TV. My son was happily occupied, so I grabbed my phone and scrolled the App Store.

There they were—my usual dating tools: OkCupid, Tinder, Bumble. All were showing the cloud icon, waiting for me to redownload.

Bumble was an immediate no. That's where I met Franco. I couldn't stomach revisiting those first messages.

Then I spotted eHarmony. A friend of mine had met someone on there recently. I'd never tried it. *Why not? Let's see how this train wreck goes.*

I downloaded the app and started answering what felt like a 2,000-question survey designed to find your perfect match. Then I hit a question that made me pause: "Do you drink?"

Every long-term relationship I'd had—my ex-husband, Franco— was impacted by addiction. Franco had been in recovery when we met. I'll never forget the heart-to-heart conversation we had in the back of a restaurant on our fourth or fifth date. After learning about what I had gone through with my ex, he came clean to me about his own history with addiction and gave me a choice as to whether or not I wanted to continue seeing him. It weighed on me for days, and after a lot of reflection, I decided I wanted to trust the man standing in front of me—clean and sober that day and multiple years before it—treating me like an absolute queen and better than any man ever had, rather than judge him based on his past. I learned the day we discovered he took his life that a secret relapse played a big role in his final decision—the police on the scene mentioned the paraphernalia they found in his apartment and my heart dropped the second I heard it. I never wanted to go through that again.

If I wanted a different outcome, the answer was clear: I don't really drink. It was true. I'd been sober on and off while on Whole30 since the day Franco died. After years of Whole30 resets, I had finally decided in 2019, following my epic, sauvignon blanc New Year's greeting meltdown that alcohol had no place in the life I was rebuilding.

I finished the survey. The app revealed my first match.

He was *cute.* Really cute. Mets fan, which is important to me, being born and raised one myself. Two boys the same ages as Franco's sons. Lived and worked in the same towns Franco did, which was weird because Long Island is not that small.

I figured, *What the hell?* and sent a little wink.

A minute later, he messaged me, "Why doesn't your profile have any pictures?"

*"Wait—what?"* I checked my profile. Sure enough, no photos. I guess they hadn't uploaded yet.

"My profile is brand-new, I just created it. They must still be processing," I typed back.

He replied instantly: "It's okay, you can send them here." He inserted a phone number.

*Who gives their number to a stranger with no photos? This guy must be a psycho!* I thought, but something in me said it was okay, so I sent the pictures.

Spoiler alert: That "psycho" became my husband.

# Why You're Ready to Give Up (and What That Really Means)

Trying again when things haven't worked out in the past takes guts, so does staying the course when you've been doing *all the right things* and still don't see results. If you're here, there's a good chance you're sitting in that messy middle:

- You've been showing up.
- You've been doing the work.
- And you're starting to wonder: *Why isn't anything changing?*

Which, let's be honest, is frustrating as hell—especially for high performers. You've vision-boarded. You've strategized. You've scheduled, journaled, manifested, action stepped, invested, meditated, and showed up on time in clean clothes (which, depending on your season of life, may be your biggest flex of all).

And yet—no breakthrough, no dramatic shift, just more effort, more waiting, more questioning, *What am I doing wrong?*

I'm a now fourth-generation entrepreneur in my family. Let me offer you a mindset shift that changed everything for me: *Entrepreneurs are literally professional failures.* We just get so good at failing, we eventually make money from it!

The same can be said of leaders, creatives, parents—anyone trying to create a life on their own terms. The ones who succeed aren't the ones who never fail. They're the ones who've learned to fail forward without losing momentum. And momentum is exactly what you need right now.

The Japanese philosophy of *Kaizen* speaks to this directly. It's the practice of making continuous, incremental improvements—tiny shifts that, over time, lead to massive transformation. Companies like Toyota credit their success to Kaizen, empowering employees at every level to identify and act on small changes that enhance efficiency and productivity.[54] And while I wasn't managing a supply chain, the principle still applied. My tiny shift—changing a single setting on a dating profile—led to the most unexpected, transformative chapter of my life.

If you're not seeing results, it doesn't always mean you're failing or that the goal is wrong, but it might mean the approach is. This is where the law of incremental increase becomes a double-edged sword: Tiny, seemingly boring daily actions *do* create transformation, but only if you're pointed in the right direction.

That's where the Lack of Consistency Culprit can trick you. You're showing up every day but to what end? If your systems, support, or strategy are out of alignment, your consistency becomes a slow burn to burnout.

That's why the bravest thing you can do in this moment may not be to keep going the way you've been; it might be to pivot. It also may require only one micro-change, not unlike my decision to say I don't drink on my dating profile surveys.

Action alone doesn't equal progress, but action plus alignment does. And sometimes, the most powerful move isn't doubling down—it's stepping back, reassessing (especially looking at data, should you have it), and asking yourself: *What's actually working? What needs to change?*

This chapter will help you answer those questions and show you how to take your next right step, even if it looks different than what you had imagined.

*Exercise*

---

# How to Pivot Without Losing Momentum

When you've been taking consistent action and still feel stuck, it's easy to spiral into self-doubt. You start to wonder:

- *Am I wasting my time?*
- *Did I set the wrong goal?*
- *Am I doing something wrong, or am I just wrong?*

Let's stop that spiral right here. If your Recap Ritual is showing the same results (or lack thereof) week after week, it's not a sign that you're broken, it's a sign that it's time to reassess. This isn't about abandoning the plan. It's about refining it.

Here are four grounded, actionable ways to pivot without losing the momentum you've worked so hard to build.

## *Step 1:* **Reassess Your Strategy**

Start with what your Recap Ritual is already trying to tell you. If you've noticed the same notes showing up week after week—"still no traction," "no change," "not working"—pay attention. That repetition is a gift. It's data. And it's your cue to pause and recalibrate.

Here's how I walk myself and my coaching clients through it:

- **Acknowledge the stall. No shame, no judgment.** Just awareness. Something isn't working—and that's okay.
- **Audit your actions.** Look at what you've *actually* done to move your goal forward. Get it all out. Make a full list.
- **Match actions to outcomes.** What's working? What's not? What's draining your time without a return?
- **Revisit your goal.** Is it still the right one, or have you outgrown it without realizing?
- **Find the gap.** Often, the missing piece reveals itself right here: a skipped step, a repeated pattern, a self-sabotage, or a habit that's quietly holding you back.
- **Brainstorm new options.** What's one small tweak that could yield a different result? (Remember the story in this chapter—one changed checkbox on a dating profile changed everything.)
- **Eliminate what's not working. Double down on what is.** This is where the 80/20 rule comes in. Let go of the 80 percent of what's keeping you busy. Focus on the 20 percent that's moving the needle—even if it's small.

## *Step 2:* **Reframe Your Progress**

Small wins count. *Let them.* Our brains are wired to look for dramatic transformation, but real change usually arrives quietly, disguised as tiny shifts:

- You say no without guilt.
- You leave the email unread until tomorrow.
- You choose the walk over the scroll.
- You pause instead of spiral.

That's growth. Don't let the absence of a breakthrough blind you to the momentum that's already building. Progress that feels small is often the most sustainable and the most worth celebrating.

That New Year's Day, it was easy to see how far I'd come simply by noticing I was actually starting to enjoy my life again. Was I fully healed? Hell no. But I could feel the progress because I was actively looking for evidence of it.

## *Step 3:* **Reinforce What's Working**

Consistency only matters when it's *aligned*. If your systems are solid and your progress is simply slow, not stalled, keep going. Keep refining. Keep stacking those small wins.

You don't need to blow everything up. When you do, that's actually a form of self-sabotage (and enough content for an entire book we don't have time to cover here). You just need to protect what's already working: your routines, rituals, habits, support systems—anything that's keeping you grounded. That's the power of compound effort. That's how professional "failures" turn momentum into mastery.

When I decided to start dating again, I realized that using dating apps had worked for me in the past—they'd led me to Franco—so of course I leaned back into what was working. That was a signal to double down, not to switch gears entirely.

## *Step 4:* **Realign with Your Vision**

Just because the *method* changes doesn't mean the *mission* does. Sometimes we resist pivoting because it feels like quitting. But there's a difference between giving up and evolving.

Just like I did that New Year's Day, ask yourself: *What's the smallest change I can make that might generate a better result?*

For me, identifying myself as sober wasn't a detour from my long-term goal, it was the most aligned step I could take toward it. It honored one of my core values, health, and reminded me that I needed to become the kind of person I was hoping to attract.

Changing your strategy doesn't mean your goal is wrong. It also doesn't mean you're changing who you are. It means you're wise enough to adjust your approach so it *actually* works. This is how you keep your foot on the gas—without burning out the engine.

## Putting It All Together

# Small Daily Actions Compound over Time

You've made it to the end of the Overwhelm Culprit framework. Since you've stuck with me this far, I want to pause here and acknowledge the journey you've taken, not just through the pages of this book but likely through a season of your life that demanded more from you than you ever expected.

You've untangled the five core culprits of overwhelm.

You've named your patterns.

You've told yourself the truth.

You've created structure and support systems where chaos once lived.

You've learned how to rebuild your foundation—slowly, intentionally, and in a way that makes space for who you're becoming.

More than anything, you've learned how to keep going when it gets hard.

And if you're like me, you've probably found that it's not the big dramatic moments that define our progress. It's the quiet ones, the steady ones, the "I don't know if this is working, but I'm going to keep trying anyway" ones. It's those small, often invisible choices—the ones no one sees—that begin to change everything.

That's what was true for me the New Year's Day when I sat on my couch, asking myself the same question I imagine you've asked at least once while reading this book: *What if nothing ever changes?* I was exhausted. I was lonely. I had done so much work—so much healing—and I still found myself questioning whether I was capable of experiencing the kind of life I envisioned for myself. But in that moment, I chose to do something small, something tiny, almost embarrassingly simple. I logged into eHarmony and adjusted one checkbox on my profile. I didn't know it yet, but that choice—the one that felt like it didn't matter—would be the catalyst for everything that came next.

Because on the other side of that checkbox was Mike.

What I couldn't have known then was that he had woken up that same morning with a similar question on his mind. After surviving his own traumatic relationship, navigating single fatherhood, and moving through the slow process of healing, he'd reached a point where he was afraid he'd never find a partner who understood what he'd been through. He had his own rules, his own protections in place. And yet, that morning, something in him shifted too.

He broke his "no pictureless profiles" rule and responded to my wink.

That was it. Two small, quiet decisions—made independently, yet rooted in the same belief: *If you want something different, you have to try something different.*

That belief would carry us through not only our early days of dating, but through one of the most pivotal global events of our lifetime. Two years later, as the world shut down during the COVID-19 pandemic, everything in our lives changed again.

We found out we were expecting a daughter. We got engaged. And before I knew it, I had gone from a single mom of one to a *married mom of four*. And here's the wildest part: It all unfolded almost exactly five years after I had first sat down and cast my original Five-Year Vision!

People often tell us how "lucky" we are. But it wasn't luck. It was the result of hundreds of tiny choices—unseen, unglamorous, and often uncomfortable—that slowly built the foundation for the life we live today. It was the product of relentless resilience, of healing and unlearning, of choosing again and again and again. And that's what I want to leave you with before we step into the final chapter.

If you've made it this far, you've already done something extraordinary. You've chosen to be honest with yourself, to examine what's not working, and to take action even when it felt unclear. You've chosen not to settle.

Now, it's time to take that momentum and channel it into something bigger, something braver, something extraordinary. Because here's another truth I want to leave you with before we move on: Extraordinary lives require extraordinary action—not once, not twice—but over and over again in the small, sacred moments when no one is watching but you.

Let's take the final step together.

*Chapter Twelve*

# Take Extraordinary Action

## Journal Entry— September 8, 2018, 8:55 PM

I missed a few days. They were really important ones too. After my last entry, we visited the cruise line's private island as well as the Atlantis Resort in the Bahamas. I didn't get to do yoga or meditate either of these days, and they both proved to be difficult for me. All I could think about was you. You and me in Mexico, how you were supposed to be there on this trip with me, then I remember you're dead. It was an awful cycle. And I was surrounded by so many seemingly happy couples. Kissing in the ocean water at the beach, holding hands, cuddling on the lazy river. I was so sad I had that experience with you in Mexico. I should have had it there, and I didn't. I loved "us." You were my other half. It's so hard for me to imagine a life with someone better, and it scares me to death.

After Atlantis, my dad yelled at me about something stupid for work, and I finally unloaded and gave him my notice. All told, he took it well, but my mother made it into the issue of the century. She said so many awful things. Calling me selfish and ungrateful. It really broke me down. Giving my notice was hard enough, but she cracked me wide open. I felt like such a failure and disappointment. During dinner, all I could think about was how I could end the pain by jumping off the ship, and that terrified me to tears. When we got out of dinner, I pretty much had a nervous breakdown and thank God I called Elizabeth. She talked me down. She also spoke to my dad and asked that everyone table the discussions until we got back. After, we had an okay few days, but I'm still depressed as fuck. My mom is also withholding watching my son as some sort of punishment.

What made me the saddest through the entire ordeal is that for the last year you were my rock to deal with these issues. I had to do this by myself. I understand now how hard it must have been for you—having now been suicidal myself—but you could have called me. I wanted to call you but instead the only person I could talk to was my therapist. I did pray to you and my guides, and that did help.

So here I am, a giant mess. I quit my job (or will soon, we still don't have my last day set). I'm depressed, and I'm terrified of what's next. I've never been this low in my life, even after my abusive marriage and divorce. I don't know what miracle I'm supposed to expect from all of this, but it better be nothing short of incredible.

> Losing you is the hardest thing I've ever experienced.
> It's like part of my soul died. I'm so afraid I'll never meet
> someone who understands or loves me like you do. It's
> not fair. I don't deserve this. I deserved to be happy, and
> I was happiest with you by my side, as selfish as that is.

I read this now, years later, and I barely recognize the woman who wrote it. But I remember exactly how she felt. She was carrying the weight of the world on her shoulders, having just made the decision to not only walk away from her safe, stable fifteen-year career but also to release the identity that career represented—one shaped by family expectation, legacy, and her own ambition.

She was deeply alone. The sting of disappointment, the ache of being seen as a failure, left her feeling hollow and isolated. As difficult as the abuse, divorce, and suicide loss had been, it was the loss of support from her family—especially the withholding of help with her child—that shook her the most. And the one person she would have turned to for comfort was now gone. Yet, that day, she chose change.

No one talks about how hard it is to change when you have to do it entirely on your own. She had spent the past year carefully building a safety net. Franco had even helped her. She'd saved over six months of emergency funds, believing it would give her the security to figure out her next move. But she didn't anticipate that the true emergency wouldn't be financial, it would be spiritual.

She didn't know what came next. Maybe she'd become a coach, like Elizabeth had suggested. Maybe she'd start a business, like the podcasters she admired online. All she knew for sure was that her soul was in crisis, and that safety net would buy her time while she waited for the miracle.

She asked for signs. Every day after meditation, she'd journal what she heard. She followed the nudges, however faint. She took aligned action even when nothing made sense.

Eventually, she negotiated a part-time consulting role to replace some income and decided to use a portion of her savings to invest in coaching. She followed an intuitive nudge after reading an online article and hired a coach she'd never met. Ironically, that same coach—seven years later—would help bring the book you're holding into the world.

Within weeks, she had her first paying clients. Within months, her story was featured in the media. She used social media like a digital journal, documenting her transformation. She built an audience of over 40,000 people. She proved, again and again, that purpose could rise from pain.

She kept following the signs. Public speaking books "fell off" bookstore shelves. Facebook ads showed her programs on speaking. Her coach dared her to apply to TEDx. At first, she laughed. But a little over a year after that cruise, she stood on a TEDx stage, the first one she had ever applied for.

Her healing extended beyond business. Therapy helped her repair relationships with her parents. She rebuilt her family. Just three months after almost jumping off a cruise ship, she opened an eHarmony account. And we all know how that turned out.

What she had done—what I had done—didn't truly hit me until after the early version of this manuscript sold to Health Communications, Inc. At first, I felt nothing. I was numb. Mike, who had witnessed every step of this journey from the very beginning, kept asking why I wasn't celebrating and I couldn't give him an answer. So I did what I always do when I feel out of alignment, I doubled down on self-care to figure out what was going on beneath the surface.

It finally hit me when I found myself in child's pose in a yoga class. The instructor said, softly, "Let them go." And just like that, I broke. I started crying uncontrollably—the kind of tears that come from deep within your bones—because in that moment, I realized what was happening. I had never mourned her, the version of me who had fought her way out of that cruise ship cabin. Who sat on the deck staring at the sun, willing herself to keep going. Who left everything familiar behind—her career, her identity, the safety net of being who everyone expected her to be. She got me here. She walked through fire to do it. And now she was gone.

Writing this book required me to become someone new. Just like she had done before. She rewrote her story after surviving abuse, divorce, and suicide loss. Now, by taking all the fear, pain, and loneliness she endured and turning it into something that can serve others, I've rewritten her story.

Both of us had to let go of who we thought we were, so we could step into who we were becoming. Whether that happened on a cruise ship or on a yoga mat, the transformation was just as real.

I've said it before, living an extraordinary life requires extraordinary action. As John F. Kennedy once said, "Things do not happen. Things are made to happen."

Here I am, writing these final words in June, exactly seven years after Franco died. Every summer, when the temperature rises and the air gets thick with humidity, my body remembers before my brain does. I find myself right back there on the lawn, staring into the sun as my tears mingled with sweat and I feel that terrible loss all over again. But now, I can see it differently.

She didn't know it at the time, but her collapse allowed the best parts of life to rush in: the deep presence she now brings to parenting; the quiet joy of real love, for a second time; the expansion of her family; and the fulfillment of a career filled with purpose. None of those things could have arrived without first letting go.

I know this won't be the last time I evolve. There will be more versions of me, more lessons, more stories to share. The difference is that I now have systems to support each transformation.

Sometimes, extraordinary action isn't flashy. Sometimes it's quiet. Sometimes it's the decision to stay—on the mat, in the room, in your life—when everything in you wants to run.

If you've made it to this point, I want you to know something: Even when life feels unsustainable, you still have a choice. Maybe it's not about the circumstances but about how long you're willing to tolerate them. When you hit rock bottom, like I did, the fear of change eventually becomes smaller than the pain of staying the same. And that's when you leap.

So now, let me ask you: What's one decision you've been putting off? And what's one extraordinary action you can take today to move toward it?

Leading an extraordinary life doesn't begin when things get easier. It begins when you take action in spite of it being difficult to act, because you believe that miracles are still possible.

I didn't get the miracle I asked for in that journal. I got something far better: I *became* the miracle . . . and so can you.

# Acknowledgments

This book was not created in isolation. It exists because of the people who stood beside me, held me up, challenged me, and reminded me—sometimes gently and sometimes firmly—that I did not have to do any of this alone.

First, I want to acknowledge my therapist, Elizabeth Franqui. Working with you quite literally changed the course of my life. From our very first session, you helped me see truths I was not yet ready to face—and gave me the support, language, and courage to act on them. The work you do matters more than you will ever know. I would not have the life I have today—the family, the career, or this book—without the foundation you helped me build. Thank you for your steadiness, your insight, and your unwavering commitment to healing.

To Franco—thank you. Our time together was short, and the loss was devastating, but I do not regret a single moment. Loving you changed me. Through you, I learned what it felt like to be fully accepted for exactly who I was, without armor or apology. That acceptance gave me safety and allowed parts of me to emerge that had been protected for decades. Though you are no longer here, the impact you had on my life—and on the woman who eventually wrote this book—remains. I carry that forward with me.

To my husband, Mike, my always and forever—meeting you when I did didn't feel possible, let alone real. You entered my life during a season when trust felt fragile, and you met me with patience, consistency, and care. You didn't just love me on my good days—you chose me on the hard ones, too. You created the space that allowed me to step back into the world, share my story, and build a business and life that reflect who I truly am. None of this exists without you. Thank you for believing in me, for supporting the work, and for showing—by example—that it is possible to love your family, love your career, love yourself, and lead well at the same time.

To my children—this book is dedicated to you. It will likely be a long time before I hand you a copy, and that's okay. Every part of this journey—every choice, every risk, every hard conversation—was shaped with you in mind. My deepest hope is that as you grow, you will never feel forced to choose between a life that matters and the people you love. Being your mom (and stepmom) is one of my greatest joys and proudest accomplishments. Thank you for being my why.

To my dad—thank you for everything you taught me, especially what leadership looks like when it's done with integrity, grit, and vision. Working alongside you for over fifteen years shaped how I think, how I lead, and how I tell stories. Walking away from the family business was one of the hardest decisions I've ever made, precisely because there was so much I loved about it. I carry the lessons with me every day.

To my mom—my resilience was modeled by you long before I had words for it. I watched you do it all—advocate fiercely, keep going when it wasn't easy, and still make space to care for yourself. During the hardest years of my life, you and Dad were there without hesitation, offering support in every form. Thank you for stepping in, especially during the messy middle, and for loving both me and my children so fully.

To Jim and Arlene, my in-laws and chosen bonus parents—thank you for the countless ways you've supported our family over the years. Your willingness to step in, help with the kids, and be part of this journey has meant more than I can express. We are so lucky to have you.

To Lauren and Jonas—thank you for decades of friendship, steady presence, and love. From the hardest chapters to the healing ones, you've been there, reminding me who I am when it mattered most.

And to Jessie—your friendship, honesty, and the conversations that helped me find my footing again were pivotal. I'm grateful for you beyond words.

Professionally, I am deeply thankful to the following people who saw my potential before I fully saw it myself:

Shannon Kaiser—thank you for being an early mentor, guide, and believer. The work we did together laid the foundation for everything that followed. Thank you for your guidance, your introductions, and for lending your voice to this book through the foreword.

Greg Faxon—thank you for helping me give language to what would become the Overwhelm Culprit framework. That moment of clarity continues to shape my work and impact.

Jess Ekstrom and the entire Mic Drop Academy team—thank you for opening the door to a path I never imagined was possible. Your belief in my story—and your encouragement to tell it fully—changed everything. The ripple effect of that support continues to reach far beyond the stage.

I also want to acknowledge the Speaker Sister community, an extraordinary group of women who became far more than peers over the years. What began as shared ambition and professional support grew into real friendship, honesty, and belonging. Through every stage of this journey, you offered perspective, encouragement, and laughter when I needed it most. The impact of that kind of community cannot be overstated, and I am deeply grateful to have walked this path alongside you.

To Denise Duffield-Thomas—your work helped me dismantle beliefs that kept me playing small for far too long. The mindset shifts I made along the way changed not only my career but my family's future. I am deeply grateful.

To my literary agent, Steve Harris—thank you for seeing the vision early and shepherding this book into the world with clarity and care. And to my editor, Christine Belleris—thank you for your trust, your guidance, and the creative freedom you gave me to tell this story honestly. Working with you has been a gift, and I can't wait to do it again.

I am also deeply grateful to the women of the Working Moms of Peloton Facebook group. More than half of the research participants for this book came from this community, and your willingness to share your experiences—honestly, vulnerably, and generously— shaped this work in profound ways. Your stories brought depth, nuance, and truth to these pages. Thank you for trusting me with them.

Finally, thank you to every woman who shared her story, her honesty, and her courage. This book carries pieces of all of you. None of this was done alone, and I hope this book reminds you that you don't have to do it alone either.

# Resources

This book is not meant to be read once and put away. It is meant to be returned to—during moments of transition, decision fatigue, burnout, or when you feel yourself slipping back into survival mode.

The following resources are included to support the ideas, data, and practices referenced throughout the book. They are not meant to be consumed all at once. Use what feels helpful for your current season, and ignore the rest for now.

## Frameworks and Core Concepts

### The Five Overwhelm Culprits

The central framework introduced in this book to help you identify the true source of overwhelm and determine where to focus your energy first:

- Lack of Clarity
- Lack of Confidence
- Lack of Community

- Lack of Conditioning
- Lack of Consistency

Each chapter includes reflection prompts and practical actions designed to help you address your current culprit without attempting to overhaul your entire life.

# Technology and Tools for Reducing Mental Load

These tools are referenced as modern supports for thinking more clearly, externalizing mental load, and creating space for better decision-making.

## ChatGPT

Used for brainstorming, thought organization, reframing challenges, and reducing cognitive overload when you feel stuck or overwhelmed: https://www.openai.com/chatgpt.

## Notion

A flexible digital workspace used to create dashboards, systems, and decision-support tools for both personal and professional life, Notion is referenced in this book as a way to externalize mental load, track priorities, and create clarity during periods of overwhelm.

Notion can be used to:

- Create personal or professional dashboards
- Organize goals, projects, and recurring responsibilities
- Track habits, energy, and patterns over time
- Centralize information to reduce decision fatigue
- Create a digital journal

When used intentionally, tools like Notion help move information out of your head and into a system—freeing up cognitive space for clearer thinking and better leadership: https://www.notion.so.

# Mindset, Meditation, and Conditioning Support

Conditioning your nervous system, mind, and body is a recurring theme throughout this book. The tools below can support that work, especially if you are building a practice from scratch.

## ThinkUp

This is a mindset and affirmation app used to support confidence-building and intentional thought work: https://www.thinkup.me.

## Insight Timer

This is a free meditation app offering beginner-friendly guided meditations, customizable timers, and community-based accountability. It is helpful for building a consistent meditation or mindfulness practice, even if you've struggled to stick with one in the past: https://insighttimer.com.

# Research, Reports, and Data Sources

The following organizations and studies are referenced throughout the book to provide data-backed context for the experiences shared. They are included to reinforce an important truth: What you are experiencing is not a personal failure. It is shaped by systems that were never designed to support women carrying both leadership and caregiving responsibilities.

## World Economic Forum (WEF)

Global gender parity, workforce participation, and leadership representation data.

- Global Gender Gap Report homepage: https://www.weforum.org/reports/global-gender-gap-report-2025/

# Deloitte—Women @ Work: A Global Outlook

Research on burnout, mental load, workplace inequity, and women's workplace experiences.

- Women @ Work global outlook hub: https://www.deloitte .com/global/en/issues/work/women-at-work.html

# Development Dimensions International (DDI)

Leadership development, transition support, and gender gaps in leader pipelines.

- Global Leadership Forecast and research hub: https://www .ddiworld.com/research/global-leadership-forecast

# OECD—Better Life Index / Well-Being Data

Global benchmarks for well-being, life satisfaction, and work-life balance.

- Better Life Index: https://www.oecdbetterlifeindex.org/
- OECD well-being data tools: https://www.oecd.org/statistics /better-life-initiative.htm

# Hays—Gender Diversity Research

Workforce equity insights based on survey data.

- Hays global gender diversity research hub: https://www.hays .com/what-we-do/diversity/gender-diversity

# Motherly—State of Motherhood

Survey-based reporting on modern motherhood, caregiving pressures, and support gaps.

- State of Motherhood report hub: https://www.mother.ly/ state-of-motherhood/

## YouGov

Public opinion and survey data referenced throughout the book.

- YouGov research hub: https://today.yougov.com/
- Careers topic and workforce data: https://today.yougov.com/topics/work

# Mental Health and Crisis Support

This book includes discussions of trauma, grief, abuse, miscarriage, and suicide loss. If any part of this book brings up distressing emotions or memories, additional support is essential.

In the United States:

988 Suicide and Crisis Lifeline

Call or text 988

https://988lifeline.org

You can find international domestic violence support resources here: https://www.hotpeachpages.net.

Working with a licensed mental health professional is strongly encouraged if you are navigating trauma, grief, anxiety, or depression.

# Domestic Abuse and Intimate Partner Violence Support

This book includes discussion of intimate partner abuse. If you are currently experiencing abuse—or questioning whether what you are experiencing is safe—support is available.

Abuse does not always look the way we expect it to. It can include emotional, psychological, financial, or physical harm, as well as patterns of control or isolation. You deserve to be safe and supported.

## In the United States:

### NATIONAL DOMESTIC VIOLENCE HOTLINE

Call: 1-800-799-SAFE (7233)

Text: START to 88788

TTY: 1-800-787-3224

https://www.thehotline.org

The National Domestic Violence Hotline offers confidential support, safety planning, and resources 24/7.

## Outside the United States:

You can find international domestic violence support resources here: https://www.hotpeachpages.net.

If you are in immediate danger, contact your local emergency number.

Seeking help does not mean you have failed. It means you are prioritizing your safety, your future, and your capacity to heal.

# Reflection and Self-Inquiry Practices

Throughout the book, you are encouraged to pause, reflect, and check in with yourself. Helpful practices include:

- Journaling or written thought downloads
- Voice notes or audio reflection
- Values clarification exercises
- Inner-child reflection prompts
- Boundary and expectation audits

There is no single "right" format. Consistency matters far more than perfection.

# Leadership Development and Ongoing Support

This book highlights the lack of leadership transition support available to women, particularly those navigating caregiving alongside ambition.

Additional support may include:

- Leadership development programs aligned with your life stage
- Coaching or advisory support during major transitions
- Mentorship or peer communities
- Skill building in communication, boundaries, and decision-making

The goal is not to do more but to build capacity in ways that are sustainable.

# Author Resources

For additional tools, speaking engagements, coaching, and resources related to the frameworks introduced in this book, visit: https://www.corrielo.com.

# A Final Note

You do not need to fix everything at once. You do not need to earn your rest. And you are not meant to carry this alone.

Use these resources as support—not as another checklist. The most important work begins with identifying what you need right now and giving yourself permission to start there.

# Endnotes


1.  Frith, Beckett, "Fathers Twice as Likely to Be Promoted as Mothers." *HR Magazine*, October 30, 2017.

2.  "Women in the Workforce Statistics 2024: Roles and Pay Gap." *TeamStage* (blog), December 24, 2021. https:/ /teamstage.io/women-in-the-workforce-statistics/.

3.  Mithani, Chabeli and Jasmine Carrazana. "Happy Equal Pay Day? Here Are 6 Charts Showing Why It's Not Much of a Celebration." *The 19th* (blog), March 14, 2023. https://19thnews.org/2023/03 /equal-pay-day-2023-charts-gender-pay-gap/.

4.  "Women Are Now a Majority of the U.S. College-Educated Labor Force | Pew Research Center." Accessed June 5, 2025. https://www.pewresearch.org/short-reads/2022/09/26/ women-now-outnumber-men-in-the-u-s-college-educated -labor-force/.

5.  "New Research: Women More Effective Than Men in All Leadership Measures." Accessed June 5, 2025. https://www

.forbes.com/sites/kevinkruse/2023/03/31/new-research
-women-more-effective-than-men-in-all-leadership
-measures/?sh=1ad20caa577a.

6.  "Women in the Workforce Statistics 2024: Roles and Pay
    Gap." *TeamStage* (blog), December 24, 2021. https:/
    /teamstage.io/women-in-the-workforce-statistics/.

7.  Orlando Health. "Pregnancy Loss: 1 in 4." Accessed June 5,
    2025. https://www.orlandohealth.com/services-and
    -specialties/orlando-health-womens-institute/content-hub
    /pregnancy-loss-1-in-4.

8.  The Hotline. "Domestic Violence Statistics." Accessed June 5,
    2025. https://www.thehotline.org/stakeholders
    /domestic-violence-statistics/.

9.  Pompili, Maurizio et al. "Bereavement after the Suicide of
    a Significant Other." *Indian Journal of Psychiatry* 55, no. 3
    (2013): 256–63. https://doi.org/10.4103/0019-5545.117145.

10. "Child Care in the U.S. Today Can Cost More Than Families
    Pay for Rent, a Mortgage or College Tuition." CBS News,
    November 26, 2024. https://www.cbsnews.com/news/child
    -care-costs-more-than-rent-in-some-u-s-counties-feds-find/.

11. "A National Profile of Sandwich Generation Caregivers
    Providing Care to Both Older Adults and Children—PMC."
    Accessed June 9, 2025. https://pmc.ncbi.nlm.nih.gov
    /articles/PMC10023280/.

12. Nagpaul, Sunny. "If You Thought Rent Was Bad, Childcare
    Now Costs More Than Housing in All 50 States," *Forbes*, May
    24 2024. Accessed June 5, 2025. . https://finance.yahoo
    .com/news/thought-rent-bad-child-care-173358694.html.

13. "In the Absence of a Village, Build Your Own—Motherly."
    Accessed June 9, 2025. https://www.motherly

/relationships/community-friendship/in-the-absence
-of-a-village-build-your-own/.

14.  "Women in Leadership Statistics: Insights for Inclusion."
Accessed June 9, 2025. https://www.ddiworld.com/blog
/women-leadership-statistics.

15.  World Economic Forum. "International Women's Day: How
the World Is Progressing on Gender Equality Across All 17
SDGs," March 6, 2024. https://www.weforum.org
/stories/2024/03/iwd24-gender-equality-sdgs/.

16.  OECD. *How's Life? 2015: Measuring Well-Being (American
Version)*. How's Life? OECD American Policy Centre, 2016.
https://doi.org/10.1787/9789264267442-ko.

17.  Liu, Jennifer. "Almost Half of Older Millennials Wish
They'd Chosen a Different Career Path—What They'd Do
Differently." CNBC, June 17, 2021. https://www.cnbc
.com/2021/06/17/nearly-half-of-older-millennials-wish
-theyd-chosen-a-different-career.html.

18.  "The Impact of Parental Influence: Career Edition | Joblist."
Accessed June 9, 2025. https://www.joblist.com/trends
/the-impact-of-parental-influence-career-edition.

19.  "Doctor, Vet, Esports Star, Influencer: Dream Jobs Among
US Teens YouGov." Accessed June 9, 2025. https://today
.yougov.com/technology/articles/39997-influencer-dream
-jobs-among-us-teens.

20.  "More Women Than Ever Are Becoming Doctors. Here's
Why There Are Still So Few." The Hill. Accessed June 9, 2025.
https://thehill.com/changing-america/respect
/equality/4479304-more-women-than-ever-are-becoming
-doctors-heres-why-there-are-still-so-few/.

21.  McLean, Carmen P., and Emily R. Anderson. "Brave Men and
Timid Women? A Review of the Gender Differences in Fear

and Anxiety." *Clinical Psychology Review* 29, no. 6 (August 1, 2009): 496–505. https://doi.org/10.1016/j .cpr.2009.05.003.

22. Gallup, Inc. "Personal Safety Fears at Three-Decade High in U.S." Gallup.com, November 16, 2023. https://news.gallup .com/poll/544415/personal-safety-fears-three-decade-high .aspx.

23. Encinas, Amaris. "Man or Bear? Hypothetical Question Sparks Conversation About Women's Safety." *USA Today*. Accessed February 1, 2025. https://www.usatoday .com/story/tech/news/2024/04/30/man-bear-tiktok -debate-explainer/73519921007/.

24. Fontana, Pat. "List of Phobias Most Common in Men | Fear and Anxiety." PACE Recovery Center, August 5, 2021. https://www.pacerecoverycenter.com/phobias -most-common-in-men/.

25. "Why Women Don't Apply for Jobs Unless They're 100 percent Qualified." Accessed June 9, 2025. https://hbr .org/2014/08/why-women-dont-apply-for-jobs-unless -theyre -100-qualified.

26. Ahmed, Aneesa. "'Out of My Mind with Grief': Britney Spears Details 2008 Breakdown in Memoir." *The Guardian*, October 19, 2023, sec. Music. https://www.theguardian.com /music/2023/oct/19/out-of-my-mind-with-grief-britney -spears-details-2008-breakdown-in-memoir.

27. Korba, Alexandra. "Charlie Sheen: A Timeline of a Troubled Life." *USA TODAY*. Accessed February 2, 2025. https:/ /www.usatoday.com/story/life/people/2015/11/16/charlie -sheen-timeline-troubled-life/75893700/.

28. Maserejian, Nancy N., Carol L. Link, Karen L. Lutfey, Lisa D. Marceau, and John B. McKinlay. "Disparities in Physicians'

Interpretations of Heart Disease Symptoms by Patient Gender: Results of a Video Vignette Factorial Experiment." *Journal of Women's Health* 18, no. 10 (October 2009): 1661–67. https://doi.org/10.1089/jwh.2008.1007.

29.  "Business Leaders Rely on Gut Instinct More Than Data | The Association of Corporate Treasurers." Accessed June 9, 2025. https://www.treasurers.org/hub/treasurer-magazine /business-leaders-rely-gut-instinct-more-data.

30.  "Only 15 Percent of People Are Self-Aware—Here's How to Change." Accessed June 11, 2025. https://www .forbes .com/sites/jeffkauflin/2017/05/10/only-15-of-people -are-self-aware-heres-how-to-change/.

31.  *How Great Leaders Inspire Action*,1272965460. https:// www.ted.com/talks/simon_sinek_how_great_leaders _inspire_action.

32.  Zippia. "15+ Essential Goal-Setting Statistics [2023]: The Importance of Setting Goals," December 11, 2023. https:/ /www.zippia.com/advice/goal-setting-statistics/.

33.  Ismail, Nick. "Lack of Female Speakers at CES: Highlighting the Gender Problem in Tech." *Information Age* (blog), January 11, 2018. https://www.information-age.com /lack-female-speakers-gender-gap-tech-9215/.

34.  Player, Abigail, Georgina Randsley de Moura, Ana C. Leite, Dominic Abrams, and Fatima Tresh. "Overlooked Leadership Potential: The Preference for Leadership Potential in Job Candidates Who Are Men vs. Women." *Frontiers in Psychology* 10 (April 16, 2019). https://doi .org/10.3389/fpsyg.2019.00755.

35.  Carnegie Mellon University. "Women Interrupted: A New Strategy for Male-Dominated Discussions—News—Carnegie Mellon University," October 21, 2020. http://www

.cmu.edu/news/stories/archives/2020/october/women
-interrupted-debate.html.

36.  Raval, Anjli. "Too Many Women Excel at Their Jobs but
     Are Ignored for Top Roles." *Financial Times*, October
     24, 2024, sec. Management. https://www.ft.com/content
     /729d1a32-62bf-4d61-b3e3-0763b7fe93ca.

37.  "Advancing the Future of Women in Business." KPMG, 2020.
     chrome-extension://efaidnbmnnnibpcajpcglclefindmkaj/
     https://assets.kpmg.com/content/dam/kpmg/sk/pdf/2020
     /2020-KPMG-Womens-Leadership-Summit-Report.pdf.

38.  Cascio, Christopher N., Matthew Brook O'Donnell, Francis
     J. Tinney, Matthew D. Lieberman, Shelley E. Taylor, Victor J.
     Strecher, and Emily B. Falk. "Self-Affirmation Activates Brain
     Systems Associated with Self-Related Processing and Reward
     and Is Reinforced by Future Orientation." *Social Cognitive and
     Affective Neuroscience* 11, no. 4 (April 2016): 621–29. https://
     doi.org/10.1093/scan/nsv136.

39.  Healthline. "Theta Brain Waves: Frequency, Sleep, Binaural
     Beats, and More," July 1, 2020. https://www.healthline.com
     /health/theta-waves.

40.  Wagoner, Mackenzie. "What We Can Learn from the
     Olympics: How to Train Your Brain Like a Champion." *Vogue*,
     August 23, 2016. https://www.vogue.com/article
     /how-to-train-your-brain-like-an-olympic-athlete-power
     -pose-mental-exercises-for-confidence.

41.  Lin, Hsiao-Hsien, Tzu-Yun Lin, Ying Ling, and Chih-
     Cheng Lo. "Influence of Imagery Training on Adjusting the
     Pressure of Fin Swimmers, Improving Sports Performance
     and Stabilizing Psychological Quality." *International Journal
     of Environmental Research and Public Health* 18, no. 22

(November 9, 2021): 11767. https://doi.org/10.3390
/ijerph182211767.

42. "Women @ Work 2023: A Global Outlook." Accessed May 5,
2025. https://www.deloitte.com/global/en/issues/work
/content/women-at-work-global-outlook-2023.html.

43. Gabrys, Robert L., Nassim Tabri, Hymie Anisman, and
Kimberly Matheson. "Cognitive Control and Flexibility in the
Context of Stress and Depressive Symptoms: The Cognitive
Control and Flexibility Questionnaire." *Frontiers in Psychology*
9 (November 19, 2018). https://doi
.org/10.3389/fpsyg.2018.02219.

44. López-Bueno, R., et al. (2022). "Physical Activity and
Mental Health in Women: A Systematic Review and Meta-
Analysis." *Preventive Medicine Reports*28 (2022): 101882.
https://www.sciencedirect.com/science/article/pii
/S2352827322002518

45. Maltagliati, Silvio, Ilyes Saoudi, Philippe Sarrazin, Stéphane
Cullati, Stefan Sieber, Aïna Chalabaev, and Boris Cheval.
"Women Carry the Weight of Deprivation on Physical
Inactivity: Moderated Mediation Analyses in a European
Sample of Adults over 50 Years of Age." SSM—*Population
Health* 20 (December 1, 2022): 101272. https://doi.org/10
.1016/j.ssmph.2022.101272.

46. Clifford, Catherine. "Bill Gates Took Solo 'Think Weeks' in a
Cabin in the Woods—Why It's a Great Strategy." CNBC, July
28, 2019. https://www.cnbc.com/2019/07/26/bill-gates-took
-solo-think-weeks-in-a-cabin-in-the-woods.html.

47. Cohen, A. L., and Gollwitzer, P. "If-Then Plans and the
Intentional Control of Thoughts, Feelings, and Actions. In N.
Sebanz and W. Prinz (eds.), *Disorders of Volition* (pp. 151–
171). *Boston Review*.

48.  "Issue Information—TOC." *Journal of Traumatic Stress* 38, no. 1 (2025): 1–3. https://doi.org/10.1002/jts.23065.

49.  "VA.Gov | Veterans Affairs." General Information. Accessed May 22, 2025. https://www.ptsd.va.gov/professional/treat /specific/ptsd_research_women.asp.

50.  Schmidt, Norman B., J. Anthony Richey, Michael J. Zvolensky, and Jon K. Maner. "Exploring Human Freeze Responses to a Threat Stressor." *Journal of Behavior Therapy and Experimental Psychiatry* 39, no. 3 (September 2008): 292–304. https://doi.org/10.1016/j.jbtep.2007.08.002.

51.  Aupperle, Robin L., Andrew J. Melrose, Murray B. Stein, and Martin P. Paulus. "Executive Function and PTSD: Disengaging from Trauma." *Neuropharmacology* 62, no. 2 (February 2012): 686–94. https://doi.org/10.1016/j .neuropharm.2011.02.008.

52.  Confino, Dan, Michal Einav, and Malka Margalit. "Post-Traumatic Growth: The Roles of the Sense of Entitlement, Gratitude and Hope." *International Journal of Applied Positive Psychology* (April 27, 2023): 1–13. https://doi.org /10.1007/s41042-023-00102-9.

53.  Wong, Y. Joel, Jesse Owen, Nicole T. Cabana, Joshua W. Brown, Sydney McInnis, Paul Toth, and Lynn Gilman. "Does Gratitude Writing Improve the Mental Health of Psychotherapy Clients? Evidence from a Randomized Controlled Trial." *Psychotherapy Research* 28, no. 2 (March 4, 2018): 192–202. https://doi.org/10.1080/10503307.2016 .1169332.

54.  Imai, M. *Kaizen: The Key to Japan's Competitive Success.* McGraw-Hill, 1986. https://global.toyota/en/company /vision-and-philosophy/production-system/.

# About the Author

Corrie LoGiudice is a keynote speaker, high-performance coach, and fourth-generation entrepreneur who helps high-achieving women—and the organizations that rely on them—turn their overwhelm into a catalyst for confident leadership. After navigating a series of life-altering events—including divorce, loss, and walking away from a senior executive role—she rebuilt her life one intentional choice at a time. Her signature Overwhelm Culprit framework was born out of that season, and the framework has since helped thousands of women clarify their next step, speak up powerfully, and lead lives that actually feel good to live.

Corrie has been featured on TEDx and in outlets *like Forbes, Thrive Global, Business Insider, Girlboss,* and more. Through her company, Corrie Lo & Co., she delivers keynotes, workshops, and coaching to powerhouse women and the companies that want to retain and grow them. Her client roster includes organizations like Michelin, Vonage, Impossible Foods, SHRM, National Grid, and dozens of women's leadership associations across the country.

Corrie lives thirty-five minutes from Manhattan and ten minutes from the beach on Long Island, New York, with her husband, four kids, two cats, and enough chaos to keep things interesting. When she's not writing or onstage, you'll find her paddleboarding, dancing, deep in a journaling spiral, or getting lost in a stack of personal development books on the beach. *The 5 Overwhelm Culprits* is her first book—and the one she wishes she had when everything fell apart.

To explore Corrie's full range of speaking topics, coaching offerings, or free tools and resources to help you navigate your Overwhelm Culprit, visit www.corrielo.com. To book Corrie for a keynote or workshop, visit the Speaking page on her site or email her team directly at team@corrielo.com.

# Praise for Corrie LoGiudice

## SPEAKING
### *Truly Outstanding*

"Through her personal story, she illustrated how individuals can continue to take action, regardless of their circumstances, and step into the leadership roles they are meant to be in. The session was not only inspiring and engaging but also demonstrated Corrie's remarkable ability to connect with the audience. She was kind enough to stay after the session to provide personalized suggestions to our attendees during the hands-on vision creation activity. I am confident that Corrie would be a valuable addition to your future events, offering your attendees a memorable and insightful experience."

—National Grid

## *Authentic, Engaging, and Entertaining*

"We were introduced to Corrie through another woman's insurance organization, and we thought she would be a perfect fit for the theme of our event, breaking barriers and cultivating greatness. Corrie's content of the 'Overwhelm Culprits' was extremely relevant and many could relate to this content on a personal level. Attendees thought Corrie was authentic, engaging, entertaining and relatable. They walked away with a true understanding of the overwhelm culprits and how to move past or combat those culprits. Corrie would be great for any organization to support their employee's growth and development. We would highly recommend Corrie to any such organization."

—Markel

## *Inspiring, Authentic, Motivating*

"I initially attended her session at a NAWIC conference and knew she would be perfect for a Michelin Women's Network Event. She is great to communicate with, and we got everything booked in a timely manner. She delivered an inspiring, authentic, and motivating message to the crowd. Highly recommend!"

—Michelin North America

## *Relatable and Appealing*

"Corrie presents her story in a relatable tone that pulls in the audience. Working with Corrie has been extremely smooth and well organized.  Her personal journey reflects why overcoming obstacles and self-reflection can guide our minds towards achieving goals. I can use her method to identify my 'Overwhelm Culprit' in many obstacles to come."

—Stop and Shop

## *Identifies with the Audience*

"She is motivating, but keeps it real, likely fueled by all of the hurdles she has successfully overcome in life. Corrie brings realism coupled with inspiration and will leave you feeling energized to tackle whatever is coming at you next."

—Executive Women International

## *Clear Message, Actionable Steps*

"Corrie Lo provided a clear message for our team to take actionable steps and conquer our overwhelm culprits! Our team enjoyed the workshop and felt it was an excellent topic for all busy women!"

—The Cook & Boardman Group

# COACHING

"I can tell you, I already got a return of 300% on my investment with Corrie and her coaching. That's only the beginning; there are other things in the pipeline that will contribute to that even more. It felt really fantastic to make a business decision like invest in coaching with Corrie and see it pay off so quickly."

—**Anna Beigelman**, licensed real estate broker

"It's just given me more confidence. I've stayed consistent with the work that I've been doing. At the start of this program, I just remember talking to Corrie about being fearful about what people are going to think, or what was going to happen, and I just started jumping in more and being like, 'Nope. I'm gonna do this. I don't really care. I know I'm good at this.'

"I have more clarity now, and I'm starting to build a foundation. It's just given me more confidence. I've stayed consistent with the work that I've been doing. I've been bringing excitement to other people which always brings me joy as well. I'm just so excited for all of those positive things that I've come to my life just from doing this program."

—**Annie Marshall**, fitness coach

"I've become much happier. I feel incredibly proud of what I've built. I've just become much happier. I'm very busy, and I'm perfectly happy to work late as long as it's on my terms. I just feel really good about everything that's happening. I'm excited to talk to more people about what I'm doing, and I feel proud, and when I look back on all my history professionally, I feel incredibly proud of what I built and that I can bring that to these smaller brands. It's just a lovely, relaxed and yet excited feeling at the same time."

—**Ariel Kochbarski**, fashion consultant